W9-CCA-221

the ICE CREAMERY COOKBOOK

RECIPES SHELLY KALDUNSKI

PHOTOGRAPHS ERIN KUNKEL

weldon**owen**

i scream, you scream...

The sound of the bell on an ice cream truck, a melting cone on a hot summer day, shared Fudgsicles in the bleachers, a sundae crowned with chocolate sauce and sprinkles—nearly everyone has at least one great ice cream memory and often more. Many of us also haven't forgotten the satisfaction of making our first-ever homemade batch of ice cream.

Today, all kinds of tools, gadgets, and ingredients are available that make it easy to put together countless ice cream concoctions at home. Although it may seem simpler to grab a pint from the grocery store or buy a cone at the local soda fountain, there's something undeniably special about whipping up a quart of your favorite flavor in your own kitchen.

Making your own ice cream allows you to both indulge in your wildest flavor dreams and control your ingredient choices and their quality. With a modern ice cream maker, turning out a batch requires little more than mixing up the custard base and then leaving it to churn in the ice cream maker while you whip up cones, toppings, and other accompaniments from scratch. Now you'll have

the time you need to give your homemade salted caramel ice cream the fudgy brownie accompaniment it deserves.

But ice cream isn't the only tasty frozen treat you'll find in these pages. This book also includes recipes for gelato, frozen yogurt, sherbet, sorbet, granita, ice pops and ice cream bars, and more. All of them are delicious when made in their traditional flavors, but they take well to the addition of modern twists, too, from lavender buds, Meyer lemon zest, and brownie bits to crushed pretzels. Whether you like your scoops classic, modern, whirled in a milkshake, frozen in a bar, or loaded with toppings, everything you need to know is here.

Once you've churned out a variety of frozen treats, some complementary sauces and toppings, and a few sweet accompaniments, it's time to celebrate with a party! Beginning on page 98, you'll find plenty of ideas—float bars, sundae smorgasbords, ice cream sandwich stations, milkshake socials—to help you host festive get-togethers guaranteed to create wonderful new ice cream memories.

introduction

ICE CREAM STYLES

French-style, or custard-style, ice cream is often called classic ice cream. Egg yolks, cream, and flavorings are cooked to make a custard, which is then churned and frozen in an ice cream maker. Philadelphia-style ice cream is made without egg yolks, so it's less rich than its French-style cousin. The lighter base works especially well for fruit ice creams because the fresh flavors of the fruit can shine through. Other ice creams that have emulsifiers as ingredients, like peanut butter, are also often made without egg yolks.

WHAT'S THE DIFFERENCE?

The presence or absence of a dairy product, or even the type of dairy used, can mean the difference between sorbet and sherbet or ice cream and gelato. Here's a guide to help you decipher the terms.

ICE CREAM Traditional ice cream is made from a mixture of a dairy product (cream or a mixture of milk and cream), a sweetener (usually granulated or brown sugar), and flavorings (like chocolate, fruit, or nuts). Many, though not all, ice creams contain egg yolks.

GELATO Soft and creamy, this Italian-style treat is traditionally made with milk, not cream, and egg yolks, though some versions include cream and exclude eggs. The signature silky texture of gelato is due less to the ingredients used than to how it is churned, in a machine that incorporates less air and freezes at a higher temperature than an ice cream maker.

FROZEN YOGURT & SHERBET A softer, tangier alternative to ice cream, frozen yogurt can be made with nonfat, low-fat, or full-fat yogurt. For creamier results, you can use Greek-style yogurt, which is higher in fat and protein than regular yogurt. Sherbet is made with a base of fruit purée and sugar to which a dairy product, such as buttermilk or cream, is added.

SORBET Sorbet is usually made from a mixture of a fruit purée, water, and sugar, which is frozen in a standard ice cream maker. Because sorbets have few other ingredients, their flavor is often quite intense.

GRANITA & ICE An Italian-style dessert, granita is made with a sugar syrup and flavorings and is frozen in a shallow pan. During the freezing process, it is scraped periodically with a fork to create a granular texture. Flavored ices are similar to granitas but often have a finer texture. Both granitas and ices can be frozen into ice pops or ice cubes.

MODERN FLAVORS

New flavors are making their way into ice cream shops across the country, adding unique and unexpected flavors to creamy scoops. It's not uncommon to find flavors such as avocado, passion fruit, basil, sea salt, curry powder, stout, or tea in your cone, sprinkled with equally inventive toppings, such as crystallized ginger and nut brittles.

CREAM OF THE CROP

Because they call for so few ingredients, the best frozen treats are made with the finest ingredients you can find. When possible, use organic dairy products, seasonal fruits, and quality spices and liqueurs.

MILK, CREAM & EGGS In these recipes, the ratio of whole milk to heavy cream is important to ensure a creamy but not too heavy texture. In some cases, ingredients such as crème fraîche or mascarpone cheese contribute creaminess, too, so the quantity of cream in the recipe is reduced. Egg yolks give French-style ice cream and gelato a luxurious mouthfeel. All of the recipes in this book use grade A large eggs. Avoid using extra-large or jumbo eggs, as they have significantly larger yolks that can throw off the results of the recipes.

FRUIT Seasonal, fresh fruits are delicious in ice creams, gelatos, frozen yogurts, and sherbets. Some fruits have high water content and can, if not cooked first or if added in excess, make frozen desserts overly icy. Cooking the fruit first reduces the amount of water added and concentrates the flavors. It's also a good way to make the most of not-quite-ripe fruits. If fruits are out of season, use high-quality, unsweetened frozen fruits.

CHOCOLATE, NUTS & OTHER FLAVORINGS Choose the best chocolate you can find; it will be creamier when melted than some lower-quality brands and will not produce a waxy sensation. Buy nuts whole and in bulk at a store where the product turnover is high. Toast or grind the nuts up to a few hours before you make the ice cream. Also, look for vanilla beans that are soft and pliable, not stiff and dry. For smooth ice creams with subtle flavor, ingredients like nuts or coffee beans are heated with the cream (and/or milk) and then removed when the cooked custard is strained. Chunkier mix-ins are often added at the end of churning.

TOPPINGS If you opt to buy your toppings and cones, hold out for your favorite brands and best-quality products. A delicious batch of homemade ice cream deserves to be accompanied by equally superior toppings, even if you don't make them from scratch.

SWEETENERS

Some form of sugar plays a role in all of the frozen treats in this book. Using the right amount of sugar is crucial: too much can inhibit freezing, making ice creams too soft and granitas slushy. For French-style ice cream, sugar is whisked with egg yolks and then dissolves during the cooking of the custard. Brown sugar is sometimes used in place of granulated sugar for a deeper flavor. Flavored sugar syrups are the bases for all the granitas and ices. Corn syrup, sometimes used in sherbets, adds creaminess and compensates for the lack of butterfat in the recipe.

introduction

TOOLS OF THE TRADE

Many types of ice cream makers are available and what you choose will depend on your budget, how often you make churned frozen desserts, and the desired quality and quantity of the finished product. Most machines will also make gelato, frozen yogurt, and sorbet.

MANUAL ICE CREAM MAKER This type of ice cream maker uses a hand crank to rotate a steel can that rests inside a large wooden bucket. A mixture of ice and rock salt is added to the space between the bucket and the steel can; the crank is then turned by hand for 20–40 minutes. It's a great way to get kids involved in the process of making ice cream, and since there's no cover, you can even let them taste the mixture after they've tried turning the crank. An electric model in the same style is also available.

ELECTRIC ICE CREAM MAKER The simplest of these machines is lightweight and comes with a canister that needs to be prefrozen for at least 24 hours before you use it. If you make ice cream often, it's a good idea to purchase two canisters, so you always have one in the freezer ready to go. Also, some stand mixer models offer a special ice cream paddle and freezable mixer bowl for making frozen desserts. More complex electric machines are equipped with built-in compression freezers, which means they are ready to churn at any time and can make batches of frozen desserts continuously. A temperature-control gauge ensures creamy, smooth results.

GELATO MAKER The primary difference between ice cream and gelato is in the way each is churned. Gelato makers freeze mixtures at a temperature that is 10–20 degrees warmer than ice cream makers. They also incorporate less air while churning, giving gelato its signature smooth, creamy texture. Unlike ice cream, gelato is best served in its soft state, directly after churning, but it can also be stored in an airtight container in a freezer for up to 3 days.

STORAGE TUBS To ensure your frozen desserts retain their just-made freshness for up to a few days, store them in durable glass storage tubs.

SCOOPS & PADDLES

A wide variety of ice cream scoops are available on the market, from the traditional no-frills metal scoops to those with release levers and some that allow you to fill the handle with water to make scooping easier. You can find most tools in a variety of sizes. Specialty paddles, used in Italy to serve gelato, are available at kitchenware stores.

These can be used to present a variety of frozen desserts in a more casual way—just pressed onto a plate or into a bowl. All types of ice cream tools benefit from a dip in cool water before scooping.

WHIPPING UP A BATCH

PREPARING THE BASE   Although the hands-on preparation time for frozen desserts is short, some steps are essential to achieving the best texture and flavor in the final product. Many recipes start by cooking a base of some kind, such as a custard or a fruit-sugar mixture. As soon as the base has finished cooking, it must be cooled immediately in an ice bath either to stop the cooking of the eggs (if making a French-style ice cream base) or to keep the fruit mixture vibrant and fresh tasting (if making a sorbet or granita base). Before churning, the cooled base must be chilled in the refrigerator until it is very cold, at least 4 hours. If the base is too warm when added to the ice cream maker, it will take longer to freeze and too much air will be incorporated, which will affect the dessert's texture and flavor.

CHURNING   To churn a frozen dessert, add the cold dessert base to the ice cream maker. Depending on the manufacturer and model, the churning will take 20–40 minutes (consult the manufacturer's instructions for specifics). When it's done, you can either serve the dessert freshly spun for a softer texture, or freeze it for at least 2 hours for firmer, scoopable results.

Swirling fresh fruit, nuts, candy, or other ingredients into frozen desserts gives them bursts of flavor and a nice texture, but the pieces must be bite size so they don't interfere with the freezing process.

STORING   To store a freshly churned frozen dessert or finished granita, spoon it into a 1- to 1½-quart freezer-safe container. Cover freshly churned desserts with parchment or waxed paper, pressing it directly onto the surface to prevent ice crystals from forming. Store in the freezer for up to 3 days.

SERVING   When ready to serve, if the frozen dessert is extremely firm, place it in the refrigerator for about 20 minutes to soften; this helps with scooping and heightens the flavors. Granitas and ices are typically served slightly thawed and slushy, so take them out of the freezer about 5 minutes before you plan to serve them. One quart of most frozen desserts will make 6–8 servings. One quart of granita or ice serves about 4. To keep desserts colder for longer, especially in hot weather, place the serving dishes in the freezer for about an hour until they are very cold.

TROUBLESHOOTING

Wine, liqueur, and other types of alcohol add bold flavor to frozen desserts. Avoid using more than is called for in the recipe, as alcohol can inhibit freezing.

introduction

mix-ins at home

Making your own mix-in ice creams at home is easy, and chances are you already have plenty of great options—salty, sweet, crunchy, fruity—on hand. Mix-ins are typically incorporated two ways: you can fold them into the finished ice cream with a rubber spatula, or you can add them to the ice cream maker during the last minute of churning. You can even create individual flavors by inviting guests to fold whatever appeals to them into their own serving. Some of the following suggestions work well as toppings, too.

SWEET

Barks and brittles

Candies (malted milk balls, licorice, gummies)

Caramel corn

Cereal

Chocolate chips

Citrus zest

Cookies (crushed or used to sandwich scoops)

Dried fruits

Fresh fruits (bananas, stone fruits)

Fruit jams

Fresh or frozen berries

Granola

Preserved fruits (lemons, figs)

SAVORY

Bacon (fried, then crumbled)

Nut butters

Plain or salted nuts (crushed)

Popcorn

Potato chips

Pretzels

Seeds (poppy seeds, pepitas, sunflower seeds)

CONDIMENTS, SPICES & MORE

Alcohol (dark, syrupy types like
    Grand Marnier or Kahlúa)

Brewed coffee or espresso

Brewed tea

Balsamic vinegar

Ground cinnamon

Heavy cream (whipped or poured on top)

Honey

Olive oil

Maldon or other flake sea salt

Maple syrup

Multicolored peppercorns

Hot chili sauce

easy diy ideas

Use leftover pie or cake as the base for
a sundae or crumble it for a topping.

Top a flour tortilla with small scoops of
ice cream, roll up, and drizzle with chocolate sauce.

For a homemade hard shell topping, melt together
2 parts coconut oil and 3 parts semisweet chocolate chips.

ICE CREAMS and GELATOS

espresso ice cream 20

STRAWBERRY ICE CREAM 23

FRESH MINT ICE CREAM WITH
CHOCOLATE FLAKES 24

VANILLA BEAN ICE CREAM 26

rich chocolate ice cream 27

CINNAMON–BROWN SUGAR ICE CREAM 28

SALTED CARAMEL ICE CREAM 31

CHOCOLATE–PEANUT BUTTER ICE CREAM 32

mexican chocolate ice cream 33

OLIVE OIL ICE CREAM WITH MEYER LEMON ZEST 35

ORANGE-CARDAMOM ICE CREAM 36

MALTED MILK CHOCOLATE ICE CREAM 37

salted peanut butter & jelly ice cream 38

GREEN TEA ICE CREAM 40

TOASTED PISTACHIO GELATO 41

CHOCOLATE–COCONUT GELATO 43

pumpkin-pumpkin with spiced pepitas 44

MASCARPONE-HAZELNUT GELATO 46

WHITE CHOCOLATE GELATO 47

CREAM CHEESE GELATO 49

Even though the custard in this recipe is strained, bits of ground espresso make their way through the sieve, giving the ice cream a welcome crunch. For a smooth variation, replace the ground coffee with ¼ cup whole espresso beans. The beans are strained out when you strain the cooked custard.

1¾ cups heavy cream

1½ cups whole milk

2 tablespoons ground espresso

4 large egg yolks

½ cup plus 2 tablespoons sugar

¼ teaspoon salt

MAKES ABOUT 1 QUART

ESPRESSO CHIP ICE CREAM

Add 5 ounces of finely grated bittersweet chocolate to the ice cream during the last minute of churning.

ESPRESSO ICE CREAM

WITH CHOCOLATE FLAKES

In a heavy saucepan, combine the cream, milk, and espresso. Warm over medium-high heat, stirring occasionally, until the mixture barely comes to a simmer, about 5 minutes.

Meanwhile, in a heatproof bowl, combine the egg yolks, sugar, and salt. Whisk vigorously until the mixture lightens in color and doubles in volume, about 2 minutes.

Remove the cream mixture from the heat. Whisking constantly, slowly pour about 1 cup of the warm cream mixture into the egg mixture and whisk until smooth. Pour the resulting egg-cream mixture back into the saucepan, whisking constantly, and place over medium heat. Using a wooden spoon, stir until the mixture forms a custard thick enough to coat the back of the spoon, 1–2 minutes. Do not let it boil.

Meanwhile, set up an ice bath in a large bowl and nest a smaller heatproof bowl inside. Pour the warm custard through a fine-mesh sieve into the smaller bowl; stir occasionally until cool. Remove the bowl from the ice bath and cover with plastic wrap. Refrigerate until very cold, at least 4 hours or up to 3 days.

Pour the cold custard into an ice cream maker and churn according to the manufacturer's instructions. Spoon the ice cream into a freezer-safe container and place parchment or waxed paper directly on the surface. Cover tightly and freeze until firm, at least 2 hours or up to 3 days.

This recipe combines the richness of a custard-based ice cream with the vibrancy of fresh strawberries, which are brightened with a touch of lemon juice. Crushing the berries instead of puréeing them creates juicy bits of strawberry flavor in each bite of ice cream.

STRAWBERRY ICE CREAM

WITH BALSAMIC STRAWBERRIES

In a bowl, toss the berries with the 2 tablespoons sugar and the lemon juice, then lightly crush with a fork. Cover and let stand for about 1 hour.

In a heavy saucepan, combine the cream and half-and-half. Warm over medium-high heat, stirring occasionally, until the mixture barely comes to a simmer, about 5 minutes. Meanwhile, in a heatproof bowl, combine the egg yolks, the remaining ⅔ cup sugar, and the salt. Whisk vigorously until the mixture lightens in color and doubles in volume, about 2 minutes.

Remove the cream mixture from the heat. Whisking constantly, slowly pour about 1 cup of the warm cream mixture into the egg mixture and whisk until smooth. Pour the resulting egg-cream mixture back into the saucepan, whisking constantly, and place over medium heat. Using a wooden spoon, stir until the mixture forms a custard thick enough to coat the back of the spoon, 1–2 minutes. Do not let it boil.

Meanwhile, set up an ice bath in a large bowl and nest a smaller heatproof bowl inside. Pour the custard through a fine-mesh sieve into the smaller bowl; stir occasionally until cool. Remove the bowl from the ice bath, stir in the strawberry mixture, and cover with plastic wrap. Refrigerate until very cold, at least 4 hours or up to 1 day.

Pour the cold custard into an ice cream maker and churn according to the manufacturer's instructions. Spoon the ice cream into a freezer-safe container and place parchment or waxed paper directly on the surface. Cover tightly and freeze until firm, at least 2 hours or up to 3 days.

3 cups strawberries
(1½ pints), hulled and
cut in half

⅔ cup plus 2 tablespoons
sugar

2 teaspoons fresh
lemon juice

1 cup heavy cream

1 cup half-and-half

3 large egg yolks

Pinch of salt

MAKES ABOUT 1½ QUARTS

BALSAMIC STRAWBERRIES

In a small saucepan, combine 2 tablespoons each sugar and balsamic vinegar. Bring to a boil over medium-high heat, stirring occasionally until the sugar is completely dissolved and a syrup forms. Remove from the heat and stir in 2 cups (1 pint) strawberries, hulled and halved. Serve warm with the Strawberry Ice Cream.

ice creams and gelatos

Using fresh mint rather than mint extract adds a bright flavor to this ice cream. Instead of mixing in large chocolate chunks, which can be both hard to bite into and difficult to scoop, the chocolate is finely grated, creating thin shards that melt easily when you eat the ice cream.

1¾ cups heavy cream

1½ cups whole milk

¾ cup fresh mint leaves

4 large egg yolks

¾ cup sugar

⅛ teaspoon salt

2 drops green food coloring (optional)

5 ounces bittersweet chocolate, finely grated

MAKES ABOUT 1 QUART

MALTED MINT ICE CREAM

Add 4 handfuls of malted milk balls, crushed into small pieces, to the ice cream during the last minute of churning.

FRESH MINT ICE CREAM WITH CHOCOLATE FLAKES

WITH MALTED MILK BALLS

In a heavy saucepan, combine the cream, milk, and mint leaves. Warm over medium-high heat, stirring occasionally, until the mixture barely comes to a simmer, about 5 minutes. Meanwhile, in a heatproof bowl, combine the egg yolks, sugar, and salt. Whisk vigorously until the mixture lightens in color and doubles in volume, about 2 minutes.

Remove the cream mixture from the heat. Whisking constantly, slowly pour about 1 cup of the warm cream mixture into the egg mixture and whisk until smooth. Pour the resulting egg-cream mixture back into the saucepan, whisking constantly, and place over medium heat. Using a wooden spoon, stir until the mixture forms a custard thick enough to coat the back of the spoon, 1–2 minutes. Do not let it boil.

Meanwhile, set up an ice bath in a large bowl and nest a smaller heatproof bowl inside. Pour the custard through a fine-mesh sieve into the smaller bowl; stir occasionally until cool. Remove the bowl from the ice bath; stir in the food coloring, if using, and cover with plastic wrap. Refrigerate until very cold, at least 4 hours or up to 3 days.

Pour the cold custard into an ice cream maker and churn according to the manufacturer's instructions. Add the grated chocolate during the last minute of churning. Spoon the ice cream into a freezer-safe container and place parchment or waxed paper directly on the surface. Cover tightly and freeze until firm, at least 2 hours or up to 3 days.

Steeping the vanilla bean pod and its seeds in the cream gives this ice cream an intense vanilla flavor and a classic speckled appearance. For a more old-fashioned approach, replace the vanilla bean with 1 tablespoon high-quality vanilla extract, stirring it into the custard just before you refrigerate it.

2 cups half-and-half

1½ cups heavy cream

1 vanilla bean, split in half lengthwise, seeds scraped

8 large egg yolks

¾ cup sugar

¼ teaspoon salt

MAKES ABOUT 1½ QUARTS

VANILLA BEAN ICE CREAM

WITH LAVENDER

In a heavy saucepan, combine the half-and-half, cream, and vanilla bean pod and seeds. Warm over medium-high heat, stirring occasionally, until the mixture barely comes to a simmer, about 5 minutes. Meanwhile, in a heatproof bowl, combine the egg yolks, sugar, and salt. Whisk vigorously until the mixture lightens in color and doubles in volume, about 2 minutes.

Remove the cream mixture from the heat. Whisking constantly, slowly pour about 1 cup of the warm cream mixture into the egg mixture and whisk until smooth. Pour the resulting egg-cream mixture back into the saucepan, whisking constantly, and place over medium heat. Using a wooden spoon, stir until the mixture forms a custard thick enough to coat the back of the spoon, 1–2 minutes. Do not let it boil.

Meanwhile, set up an ice bath in a large bowl and nest a smaller heatproof bowl inside. Pour the warm custard through a fine-mesh sieve into the smaller bowl. Discard the vanilla bean. Stir the custard occasionally until cool. Remove the bowl from the ice bath and cover with plastic wrap. Refrigerate until very cold, at least 4 hours or up to 3 days.

Pour the cold custard into an ice cream maker and churn according to the manufacturer's instructions. Spoon the ice cream into a freezer-safe container and place parchment or waxed paper directly on the surface. Cover tightly and freeze until firm, at least 2 hours or up to 3 days.

LAVENDER VANILLA BEAN ICE CREAM

Add 2 tablespoons dried or 3 tablespoons fresh culinary lavender to the cream as it heats. The lavender is strained out when you strain the custard.

Using high-quality chocolate, such as Valrhona or Scharffen Berger, ensures this ice cream has a rich flavor and creamy texture. Look for a bar with 70 percent cacao solids; the higher the cacao content, the more intense the flavor. Low-quality chocolate has a waxy coating and won't achieve the desired smooth mouthfeel.

RICH CHOCOLATE ICE CREAM

WITH CACAO NIBS & SALTED CARAMEL

In a heavy saucepan, combine the cream and milk. Warm over medium-high heat, stirring occasionally, until the mixture barely comes to a simmer, about 5 minutes. Meanwhile, in a heatproof bowl, combine the egg yolks, sugar, cocoa powder, and salt. Whisk vigorously until the mixture doubles in volume, about 2 minutes.

Remove the cream mixture from the heat. Whisking constantly, slowly pour about 1 cup of the warm cream mixture into the egg mixture and whisk until smooth. Pour the resulting egg-cream mixture back into the saucepan, whisking constantly, and place over medium heat. Add the chopped chocolate and vanilla to the saucepan. Using a wooden spoon, stir until the chocolate melts and the mixture forms a custard thick enough to coat the back of the spoon, 1–2 minutes. Do not let it boil.

Meanwhile, set up an ice bath in a large bowl and nest a smaller heatproof bowl inside. Pour the warm custard through a fine-mesh sieve into the smaller bowl; stir occasionally until cool. Remove the bowl from the ice bath and cover with plastic wrap. Refrigerate until very cold, at least 4 hours or up to 3 days.

Pour the cold custard into an ice cream maker and churn according to the manufacturer's instructions. Spoon the ice cream into a freezer-safe container and place parchment or waxed paper directly on the surface. Cover tightly and freeze until firm, at least 2 hours or up to 3 days. When ready to serve, top with flaked sea salt, if using.

2 cups heavy cream

1½ cups whole milk

7 large egg yolks

¾ cup sugar

¼ cup unsweetened cocoa powder

¼ teaspoon salt

7 ounces bittersweet chocolate, finely chopped

2 teaspoons vanilla extract

Flaked sea salt, for serving (optional)

MAKES ABOUT 1½ QUARTS

CHOCOLATE-CHOCOLATE WITH SALTED CARAMEL

Have ready ¾ cup Salted Caramel Sauce (page 90). Add ¾ cup cacao nibs during the last minute of churning. Spoon half of the ice cream into the container, top with half of the sauce, and stir gently in a figure eight to create large streaks. Repeat with the remaining ice cream and sauce. Do not overmix.

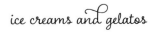

ice creams and gelatos

Using both whole cinnamon sticks and ground cinnamon intensifies the flavor in this ice cream, which recalls home-baked treats. If you only have one or the other form in your pantry, use 5 cinnamon sticks or ½ teaspoon ground cinnamon.

2 cups heavy cream

1½ cups whole milk

4 cinnamon sticks, broken into pieces

⅛ teaspoon ground cinnamon

5 large egg yolks

⅔ cup packed light brown sugar

Pinch salt

MAKES ABOUT 1½ QUARTS

BRIOCHE CINNAMON TOAST SANDWICHES

Split individual-size brioche rolls in half, butter the cut sides, and broil until the butter begins to brown and the edges are golden. Generously sprinkle both sides immediately with cinnamon sugar and fill with a scoop of Cinnamon-Brown Sugar Ice Cream.

CINNAMON–BROWN SUGAR ICE CREAM

ON BRIOCHE CINNAMON TOAST

In a heavy saucepan, combine the cream, milk, cinnamon sticks, and ground cinnamon. Warm over medium-high heat, stirring occasionally, until the mixture barely comes to a simmer, about 5 minutes. Meanwhile, in a heatproof bowl, combine the egg yolks, brown sugar, and salt. Whisk vigorously until the mixture lightens in color and doubles in volume, about 2 minutes.

Remove the cream mixture from the heat. Whisking constantly, slowly pour about 1 cup of the warm cream mixture into the egg mixture and whisk until smooth. Pour the resulting egg-cream mixture back into the saucepan, whisking constantly, and place over medium heat. Using a wooden spoon, stir until the mixture forms a custard thick enough to coat the back of the spoon, 1–2 minutes. Do not let it boil.

Meanwhile, set up an ice bath in a large bowl and nest a smaller heatproof bowl inside. Pour the warm custard through a fine-mesh sieve into the smaller bowl; stir occasionally until cool. Remove the bowl from the ice bath and cover with plastic wrap. Refrigerate until very cold, at least 4 hours or up to 3 days.

Pour the cold custard into an ice cream maker and churn according to the manufacturer's instructions. Spoon the ice cream into a freezer-safe container and place parchment or waxed paper directly on the surface. Cover tightly and freeze until firm, at least 2 hours or up to 3 days.

This ice cream has a lot of buttery-sweet caramel flavor and just a hint of saltiness, bringing a savory accent to a favorite dessert. Fine sea salt, added here to the custard base, is preferred over other types of salt for its fresh-from-the-sea flavor, small crystals, and lack of additives.

SALTED CARAMEL ICE CREAM

ON BROWNIES

In a heavy saucepan, cook the sugar over medium-high heat until it begins to melt, about 5 minutes. Continue to cook, stirring, until the sugar is melted and turns a golden amber, about 3 minutes. Stirring constantly, carefully add the butter, cream, and milk. Reduce the heat to medium and continue to cook, stirring occasionally, until the mixture is completely melted and returns to a bare simmer, about 5 minutes.

Meanwhile, in a heatproof bowl, combine the egg yolks, vanilla, and salt. Whisk vigorously until the mixture lightens in color and doubles in volume, about 2 minutes.

Remove the cream mixture from the heat. Whisking constantly, slowly pour about 1 cup of the warm cream mixture into the egg mixture and whisk until smooth. Pour the resulting egg-cream mixture back into the saucepan, whisking constantly, and place over medium heat. Using a wooden spoon, stir until the mixture forms a custard thick enough to coat the back of the spoon, 1–2 minutes. Do not let it boil.

Meanwhile, set up an ice bath in a large bowl and nest a smaller heatproof bowl inside. Pour the warm custard through a fine-mesh sieve into the smaller bowl; stir occasionally until cool. Remove the bowl from the ice bath and cover with plastic wrap. Refrigerate until very cold, at least 4 hours or up to 3 days.

Pour the cold custard into an ice cream maker and churn according to the manufacturer's instructions. Spoon the ice cream into a freezer-safe container and place parchment or waxed paper directly on the surface. Cover tightly and freeze until firm, at least 2 hours or up to 3 days.

1⅓ cups sugar

4 tablespoons salted butter

1½ cups heavy cream

1½ cups milk

6 large egg yolks

1 teaspoon vanilla extract

¾ teaspoon fine sea salt

MAKES ABOUT 1 QUART

SALTED CARAMEL ICE CREAM ON BROWNIES

Place a Fudgy Brownie (page 85) in the bottom of each bowl. Top with a scoop of Salted Caramel Ice Cream and drizzle with Salted Caramel Sauce (page 90).

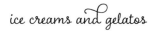

ice creams and gelatos

Here, a classic flavor pairing is transformed into an easy-to-make ice cream. Natural peanut butter is preferred for this recipe because it has an intense peanut flavor and little or no sugar added. Be sure to stir it vigorously before using to incorporate any oil on the top.

6 tablespoons unsalted butter, at room temperature

¾ cup confectioners' sugar

¾ cup crunchy natural peanut butter

3 tablespoons heavy cream

Rich Chocolate Ice Cream (page 27)

MAKES ABOUT 1¾ QUARTS

CHOCOLATE–PEANUT BUTTER ICE CREAM

> **AS FUDGE BOMBS**

In a bowl, combine the butter, confectioners' sugar, peanut butter, and cream. Using an electric mixer on medium-high speed, beat until the mixture is light and fluffy, about 5 minutes, scraping down the sides of the bowl as needed. Use right away, or spoon into an airtight container and refrigerate for up to 3 days. (If refrigerated, let stand at room temperature for about 1 hour to soften before using.)

Make the ice cream as directed. As soon as it has finished churning, spoon half of it into a freezer-safe container. Top with dollops of the peanut butter mixture, using about half of it, and stir gently in a figure eight to swirl it into the ice cream. Top with the remaining ice cream and then with the remaining peanut butter mixture and again stir in a figure eight to mix. Place parchment or waxed paper directly on the surface. Cover tightly and freeze until firm, at least 2 hours or up to 3 days.

CHOCOLATE-PEANUT BUTTER FUDGE BOMBS

Freeze the peanut butter mixture until firm, about 20 minutes. Using a small (¾-inch) scoop, scoop rounds of the mixture and place, well spaced, on a parchment paper–lined baking sheet. Using a large (2-inch) scoop, scoop rounds of the Rich Chocolate Ice Cream and place each one around a small peanut butter center. Freeze flat side down and then glaze with Hot Fudge Sauce (page 89).

The intense flavor of this ice cream comes from using two types of chocolate and hot chiles, which add an unexpected kick. Cinnamon sticks and star anise pods also contribute hints of spice. The use of brown sugar, rather than granulated sugar, deepens the overall flavor.

MEXICAN CHOCOLATE ICE CREAM

In a heavy saucepan, combine the cream, milk, chiles, cinnamon sticks, and star anise. Warm over medium-high heat, stirring occasionally, until the mixture barely comes to a simmer, about 5 minutes. Meanwhile, in a heatproof bowl, combine the egg yolks, brown sugar, vanilla, and salt. Whisk vigorously until the mixture lightens in color and doubles in volume, about 2 minutes.

Remove the cream mixture from the heat. Whisking constantly, slowly pour about 1 cup of the warm cream mixture into the egg mixture and whisk until smooth. Pour the resulting egg-cream mixture back into the saucepan, whisking constantly, and place over medium heat. Add the bittersweet and unsweetened chocolates. Using a wooden spoon, stir until the chocolate has melted and the mixture forms a custard thick enough to coat the back of the spoon, 1–2 minutes. Do not let it boil.

Meanwhile, set up an ice bath in a large bowl and nest a smaller heatproof bowl inside. Pour the warm custard through a fine-mesh sieve into the smaller bowl; stir occasionally until cool. Remove the bowl from the ice bath and cover with plastic wrap. Refrigerate until very cold, at least 4 hours or up to 3 days.

Pour the cold custard into an ice cream maker and churn according to the manufacturer's instructions. Spoon the ice cream into a freezer-safe container and place parchment or waxed paper directly on the surface. Cover tightly and freeze until firm, at least 2 hours or up to 3 days.

1¾ cups heavy cream

1½ cups whole milk

2 dried red chiles, stemmed and seeded, or ¼ teaspoon cayenne pepper

3 cinnamon sticks

3 star anise pods

4 large egg yolks

⅔ cup packed light brown sugar

2 teaspoons vanilla extract

¼ teaspoon salt

4 ounces bittersweet chocolate, finely chopped

1 ounce unsweetened chocolate, finely chopped

MAKES ABOUT 1 QUART

ice creams and gelatos

Plenty of egg yolks and a deep golden olive oil tint this ice cream a beautiful pale yellow. Warming the Meyer lemon zest with the cream and milk gives the custard a sweet, bright taste and a delicate perfume, and silky olive oil lends its unique flavor and luxurious mouthfeel.

OLIVE OIL ICE CREAM WITH MEYER LEMON ZEST

In a heavy saucepan, combine the milk, cream, and lemon zest. Warm over medium-high heat, stirring occasionally, until the mixture barely comes to a simmer, about 5 minutes. Meanwhile, in a heatproof bowl, combine the egg yolks, sugar, and salt. Whisk vigorously until the mixture lightens in color and doubles in volume, about 2 minutes.

Remove the milk mixture from the heat. Whisking constantly, slowly pour about 1 cup of the warm milk mixture into the egg mixture and whisk until smooth. Pour the resulting egg-milk mixture back into the saucepan, whisking constantly, and place over medium heat. Using a wooden spoon, stir until the mixture forms a custard thick enough to coat the back of the spoon, 1–2 minutes. Do not let it boil.

Meanwhile, set up an ice bath in a large bowl and nest a smaller heatproof bowl inside. Pour the warm custard through a fine-mesh sieve into the smaller bowl; stir occasionally until cool. Remove the bowl from the ice bath, stir in the olive oil, and cover with plastic wrap. Refrigerate until very cold, at least 4 hours or up to 3 days.

Pour the cold custard into an ice cream maker and churn according to the manufacturer's instructions. Spoon the ice cream into a freezer-safe container and place parchment or waxed paper directly on the surface. Cover tightly and freeze until firm, at least 2 hours or up to 3 days. When ready to serve, scoop into bowls and drizzle each serving with olive oil.

1½ cups whole milk

1¼ cups heavy cream

Grated zest of 2 Meyer lemons

7 large egg yolks

⅔ cup sugar

Pinch salt

⅓ cup extra-virgin olive oil, plus more for serving

MAKES ABOUT 1 QUART

ice creams and gelatos

Whole cardamom pods and orange zest are infused into a rich custard base for an elegant spiced ice cream. This is the perfect finale for a dinner party—the flavor is sophisticated yet the dessert can be made days in advance. Garnish servings with candied orange peel.

2 cups heavy cream

1½ cups whole milk

2 tablespoons cardamom pods, toasted (see below) and crushed with a heavy saucepan

Grated zest of 1 orange

5 large egg yolks

¾ cup sugar

¼ teaspoon salt

MAKES ABOUT 1½ QUARTS

ORANGE-CARDAMOM ICE CREAM

In a heavy saucepan, combine the cream, milk, cardamom, and orange zest. Warm over medium-high heat, stirring occasionally, until the mixture barely comes to a simmer, about 5 minutes. Meanwhile, in a heatproof bowl, combine the egg yolks, sugar, and salt. Whisk vigorously until the mixture lightens in color and doubles in volume, about 2 minutes.

Remove the cream mixture from the heat. Whisking constantly, slowly pour about 1 cup of the warm cream mixture into the egg mixture and whisk until smooth. Pour the resulting egg-cream mixture back into the saucepan, whisking constantly, and place over medium heat. Using a wooden spoon, stir until the mixture forms a custard thick enough to coat the back of the spoon, 1–2 minutes. Do not let it boil.

Meanwhile, set up an ice bath in a large bowl and nest a smaller heatproof bowl inside. Pour the warm custard through a fine-mesh sieve into the smaller bowl; stir occasionally until cool. Remove from the ice bath and cover with plastic wrap. Refrigerate until very cold, at least 4 hours or up to 3 days.

Pour the cold custard into an ice cream maker and churn according to the manufacturer's instructions. Spoon the ice cream into a freezer-safe container and place parchment or waxed paper directly on the surface. Cover tightly and freeze until firm, at least 2 hours or up to 3 days.

TOASTED CARDAMOM PODS: Toasting the cardamom pods before crushing them enhances their earthy flavor. In a dry frying pan over medium-low heat, toast the cardamom pods, tossing frequently, until fragrant, about 2 minutes. Transfer to a plate and let cool completely.

ice creams and gelatos

Classic soda-fountain flavors combine in this ice cream, satisfying the child in all of us. Malted milk powder is easy to find at most grocery stores; look for it in the baking aisle. Because the milk powder is very sweet, only a small amount of sugar is called for here.

MALTED MILK CHOCOLATE ICE CREAM

In a heavy saucepan, combine the milk, cream, and milk powder. Warm over medium-high heat, stirring occasionally, until the mixture barely comes to a simmer, about 5 minutes. Meanwhile, in a bowl, combine the egg yolks, sugar, cocoa powder, and salt. Whisk vigorously until the mixture lightens in color and doubles in volume, about 2 minutes.

Remove the milk mixture from the heat. Whisking constantly, slowly pour about 1 cup of the milk mixture into the egg mixture and whisk until smooth. Pour the resulting egg-milk mixture back into the saucepan, whisking constantly, and place over medium heat. Add the chocolate. Using a wooden spoon, stir until the chocolate has completely melted and the mixture forms a custard thick enough to coat the back of the spoon, 1–2 minutes. Do not let it boil.

Meanwhile, set up an ice bath in a large bowl and nest a smaller heatproof bowl inside. Pour the warm custard through a fine-mesh sieve into the smaller bowl; stir occasionally until cool. Remove the bowl from the ice bath and cover with plastic wrap. Refrigerate until very cold, at least 4 hours or up to 3 days.

Pour the cold custard into an ice cream maker and churn according to the manufacturer's instructions. Spoon the ice cream into a freezer-safe container and place parchment or waxed paper directly on the surface. Cover tightly and freeze until firm, at least 2 hours or up to 3 days.

1½ cups whole milk

1½ cups heavy cream

½ cup malted milk powder or chocolate malt powder

4 large egg yolks

⅓ cup sugar

2 tablespoons unsweetened cocoa powder

¼ teaspoon salt

5 ounces milk chocolate, finely chopped

MAKES ABOUT 1 QUART

ice creams and gelatos

Savory and sweet collide in this adult variation on a childhood classic. Resist overmixing the jam into the peanut butter ice cream. You want large streaks of fruity sweetness to balance that salty peanut flavor. Top with chopped peanuts for extra crunch.

1½ cups heavy cream

1½ cups whole milk

1½ cups smooth salted natural peanut butter

¾ cup light corn syrup

⅓ cup sugar

Pinch salt

1 cup Concord grape jam (or desired flavor)

MAKES ABOUT 1½ QUARTS

SALTED PEANUT BUTTER & JELLY ICE CREAM

WITH SALTINE CRUNCH

In a bowl, whisk together the cream, milk, peanut butter, corn syrup, sugar, and salt. Cover and refrigerate until very cold, at least 2 hours or up to 1 day.

Pour the cold peanut butter mixture into an ice cream maker and churn according to the manufacturer's instructions. As soon as the ice cream has finished churning, spoon half of it into a freezer-safe container. Top with dollops of the grape jam, using about half of it, and stir gently in a figure eight to swirl it into the ice cream. Top with the remaining ice cream and then with the remaining jam and again stir in a figure eight to mix.

Place parchment or waxed paper directly on the surface. Cover tightly and freeze until firm, at least 2 hours or up to 3 days.

PEANUT BUTTER & JELLY SALTINE CRUNCH ICE CREAM

Crush 10 saltine crackers. After churning, add the crackers in two additions, with the grape jam, stirring gently in a figure eight swirl after each addition.

The floral flavor of green tea pairs nicely with semisweet chocolate. If you are unable to find green tea powder, 3 green tea bags can be used in its place. Heat the half-and-half and cream until they come to a simmer; remove from the heat, add the tea bags, and steep for 5 minutes. Discard the tea bags.

2 cups half-and-half

1½ cups heavy cream

1 tablespoon matcha green tea powder

4 large egg yolks

¾ cup sugar

Pinch salt

MAKES ABOUT 1 QUART

GREEN TEA ICE CREAM WITH CHOCOLATE SLIVERS

Melt 4 ounces chopped semisweet chocolate. Pour onto a parchment-lined baking sheet and spread paper-thin with an offset spatula. Refrigerate until firm, about 10 minutes. Break into bite-size pieces and refrigerate until needed. Add to the ice cream during the last minute of churning.

GREEN TEA ICE CREAM

WITH CHOCOLATE SLIVERS

In a heavy saucepan, combine the half-and-half, cream, and tea. Warm over medium-high heat, stirring occasionally, until the mixture barely comes to a simmer, about 5 minutes. Meanwhile, in a heatproof bowl, combine the egg yolks, sugar, and salt. Whisk vigorously until the mixture lightens in color and doubles in volume, about 2 minutes.

Remove the cream mixture from the heat. Whisking constantly, slowly pour about 1 cup of the warm cream mixture into the egg mixture and whisk until smooth. Pour the resulting egg-cream mixture back into the saucepan, whisking constantly, and place over medium heat. Using a wooden spoon, stir until the mixture forms a custard thick enough to coat the back of the spoon, 1–2 minutes. Do not let it boil.

Meanwhile, set up an ice bath in a large bowl and nest a smaller heatproof bowl inside. Pour the warm custard through a fine-mesh sieve into the smaller bowl; stir occasionally until cool. Remove the bowl from the ice bath and cover with plastic wrap. Refrigerate until very cold, at least 4 hours or up to 3 days.

Pour the cold custard into an ice cream maker and churn according to the manufacturer's instructions. Spoon the ice cream into a freezer-safe container and place parchment or waxed paper directly on the surface. Cover tightly and freeze until firm, at least 2 hours or up to 3 days.

To toast the pistachios, place the shelled pistachios in a single layer on a rimmed baking sheet and bake in a preheated 350°F oven until fragrant, about 10 minutes.

TOASTED PISTACHIO GELATO

WITH HONEY SWIRL

In a heavy saucepan, combine the milk and pistachios. Warm over medium-high heat, stirring occasionally, until the mixture barely comes to a simmer, about 5 minutes. Meanwhile, in a heatproof bowl, combine the egg yolks, sugar, and salt. Whisk vigorously until the mixture lightens in color and doubles in volume, about 2 minutes.

Remove the milk mixture from the heat. Whisking constantly, slowly pour about 1 cup of the warm milk mixture into the egg mixture and whisk until smooth. Pour the resulting egg-milk mixture back into the saucepan, whisking constantly, and place over medium heat. Using a wooden spoon, stir until the mixture forms a custard thick enough to coat the back of the spoon, 1–2 minutes. Do not let it boil.

Meanwhile, set up an ice bath in a large bowl and nest a smaller heatproof bowl inside. Pour the custard through a fine-mesh sieve into the smaller bowl; stir occasionally until cool. Remove the bowl from the ice bath; stir in the almond extract and the food coloring, if using; and cover with plastic wrap. Refrigerate until very cold, at least 4 hours or up to 3 days.

Pour the cold custard into an ice cream maker and churn according to the manufacturer's instructions. Serve the gelato right away, or spoon it into a freezer-safe container, place parchment or waxed paper directly on the surface, cover tightly, and freeze for up to 3 days.

PISTACHIO GELATO POPS: To make single servings, use a 1½-inch scoop to form rounds of firm gelato and place them on a parchment paper–lined baking sheet. Insert a craft stick about 1 inch into each scoop, then dip the top half of each pop into chopped toasted pistachios. Freeze until serving.

5 cups whole milk

2 cups unsalted shelled pistachios, toasted (see above) and coarsely chopped

10 large egg yolks

1½ cups sugar

¼ teaspoon salt

1 teaspoon almond extract

2–3 drops green food coloring (optional)

MAKES ABOUT 1½ QUARTS

TOASTED PISTACHIO GELATO WITH HONEY SWIRL

Have ready ¾ cup wildflower honey. Spoon one-third of the ice cream into the container, top with one-third of the honey, and stir gently in a figure eight to create large streaks. Repeat with the remaining ice cream and honey in two batches. Do not overmix.

ice creams and gelatos

This gelato is vegan, though you would never guess it by the rich and full mouthfeel that good-quality dark chocolate and coconut milk provide. When churned in an ice cream machine the texture is creamy and luscious, as if actual cream were included in the recipe.

CHOCOLATE-COCONUT GELATO

WITH DIPPED BARS VARIATION

In a heavy saucepan, combine the sugar, coconut water, and cocoa powder and bring to a boil over medium-high heat, stirring occasionally until the sugar and cocoa powder are completely dissolved and a syrup has formed. Remove from the heat and add the chocolate, stirring until completely melted. Add the coconut milk, rum, and salt and stir well. Let cool to room temperature.

Pour the cooled mixture into a blender or food processor and process until very smooth. Transfer to a bowl, cover, and refrigerate until very cold, at least 2 hours or up to 1 day.

Pour the cold mixture into an ice cream maker and churn according to the manufacturer's instructions. Serve the gelato right away, or spoon it into a freezer-safe container, place parchment or waxed paper directly on the surface, cover tightly, and freeze for up to 3 days.

1 cup sugar

1 cup coconut water

1 tablespoon unsweetened cocoa powder

6 ounces bittersweet chocolate such as Scharffen Berger or Valrhona, finely chopped

2 cups coconut milk

1 tablespoons dark rum

Pinch of salt

MAKES ABOUT 1 QUART

CHOCOLATE-DIPPED CHOCOLATE-COCONUT BARS

Freeze the gelato in an ice cream bar mold until solid, at least 2 hours or up to 3 days. Unmold the frozen bars and dip the top halves into 8 ounces melted bittersweet chocolate, then coat the chocolate with ½ cup finely shredded dried coconut.

Here, the rich pumpkin flavor of the ice cream is enhanced by a trio of fall spices. When paired with a scoop of Cream Cheese Gelato (page 49), the result is reminiscent of frozen pumpkin cheesecake. For an elegant dessert, top with coarsely chopped crystallized ginger in place of the pepitas.

1 cup pumpkin purée

1 cup heavy cream

2½ cups half-and-half

6 large egg yolks

¾ cup packed dark brown sugar

½ teaspoon ground cinnamon

½ teaspoon ground ginger

Pinch freshly grated nutmeg

¼ teaspoon salt

Spiced Pepitas (page 94)

MAKES ABOUT 1½ QUARTS

PUMPKIN-PUMPKIN WITH SPICED PEPITAS

In a heavy saucepan, combine the pumpkin, cream, and half-and-half. Warm over medium-high heat, stirring occasionally, until the mixture barely comes to a simmer, about 5 minutes. Meanwhile, in a heatproof bowl, combine the egg yolks, sugar, cinnamon, ginger, nutmeg, and salt. Whisk vigorously until the mixture lightens in color and doubles in volume, about 2 minutes.

Remove the pumpkin mixture from the heat. Whisking constantly, slowly pour about 1 cup of the warm pumpkin mixture into the egg mixture and whisk until smooth. Pour the resulting egg-pumpkin mixture back into the saucepan, whisking constantly, and place over medium heat. Using a wooden spoon, stir until the mixture forms a custard thick enough to coat the back of a spoon, 1–2 minutes. Do not let it boil.

Meanwhile, set up an ice bath in a large bowl and nest a smaller heatproof bowl inside. Pour the warm custard through a fine-mesh sieve into the smaller bowl; stir occasionally until cool. Remove the bowl from the ice bath and cover with plastic wrap. Refrigerate until very cold, at least 4 hours or up to 3 days.

Pour the cold custard into an ice cream maker and churn according to the manufacturer's instructions. Spoon the ice cream into a freezer-safe container and place parchment paper or waxed paper directly on the surface. Cover tightly and freeze until firm, at least 2 hours or up to 3 days.

To serve, scoop the ice cream into bowls and top with the Spiced Pepitas.

The richness of this gelato comes from the high amount of butterfat in the mascarpone cheese used in place of the usual egg yolks. The creamy, semisweet base is the perfect showcase for the intensely nutty hazelnuts in this Italian-influenced treat.

1 cup hazelnuts

1 cup whole milk

1 cup heavy cream

¾ cup sugar

12 ounces mascarpone cheese

½ teaspoon vanilla extract

Pinch salt

MAKES ABOUT 1 QUART

MASCARPONE-HAZELNUT GELATO

Preheat the oven to 350°F. Spread the hazelnuts on a rimmed baking sheet and bake until golden, about 10 minutes, rotating the sheet 180 degrees about halfway through the baking time. While the nuts are still warm, rub them with a kitchen towel to remove the skins. Let cool completely.

In a blender or food processor, combine the hazelnuts, milk, cream, sugar, mascarpone, vanilla, and salt and blend until smooth. Pour into a bowl, cover, and refrigerate until very cold, at least 2 hours or up to 1 day.

Pour the cold cream mixture into an ice cream maker and churn according to the manufacturer's instructions. As soon as it looks like softly whipped cream, remove the gelato from the ice cream maker; mascarpone can become grainy if overwhipped. Serve the gelato right away, or spoon it into a freezer-safe container, place parchment or waxed paper directly on the surface, cover tightly, and freeze for up to 3 days.

White chocolate is very sweet, so it pairs nicely with tart fruit and tangy sauces, such as the Fresh Strawberry Topping (page 89). Because adding white chocolate to the custard base speeds up the cooking time, you must watch the custard closely as it cooks and take extra care that it doesn't burn.

WHITE CHOCOLATE GELATO

WITH PRETZELS

In a heavy saucepan over medium-high heat, gently warm the milk, stirring occasionally, until it barely comes to a simmer, about 5 minutes. Meanwhile, in a heatproof bowl, combine the egg yolks, sugar, vanilla, and salt. Whisk vigorously until the mixture lightens in color and doubles in volume, about 2 minutes.

Remove the milk from the heat. Whisking constantly, slowly pour about 1 cup of the warm milk into the egg mixture and whisk until smooth. Pour the resulting egg-milk mixture back into the saucepan, whisking constantly, and place over medium heat. Add the white chocolate and stir with a wooden spoon until the chocolate is completely melted and the mixture forms a custard thick enough to coat the back of the spoon, 1–2 minutes. Do not let it boil.

Meanwhile, set up an ice bath in a large bowl and nest a smaller heatproof bowl inside. Pour the warm custard through a fine-mesh sieve into the smaller bowl; stir occasionally until cool. Remove the bowl from the ice bath and cover with plastic wrap. Refrigerate until very cold, at least 4 hours or up to 3 days.

Pour the cold custard into an ice cream maker and churn according to the manufacturer's instructions. Serve the gelato right away, or spoon it into a freezer-safe container, place parchment or waxed paper directly on the surface, cover tightly, and freeze for up to 3 days.

2½ cups whole milk

5 large egg yolks

⅔ cup sugar

½ teaspoon vanilla extract

¼ teaspoon salt

7 ounces white chocolate, finely chopped

MAKES ABOUT 1 QUART

WHITE CHOCOLATE–PRETZEL GELATO

Add 2 cups crushed salted pretzels during the last minute of churning.

ice creams and gelatos

This gelato will make you think of frozen cheesecake. Classic and delicious on its own, enjoy it sandwiched between two graham crackers, or after the gelato has been churned, experiment with swirling in your favorite items. Balsamic strawberries (page 23) are especially tasty.

CREAM CHEESE GELATO

ON GRAHAM CRACKERS

In a heavy saucepan, combine the sugar, milk, and corn syrup. Warm over medium-high heat, stirring occasionally, until the mixture barely comes to a simmer, about 5 minutes. Remove from the heat and whisk in the cream cheese, vanilla, and salt. Let the mixture cool, then transfer to a blender or food processor and process until smooth. Pour into a bowl, cover, and refrigerate until very cold, at least 2 hours or up to 1 day.

Pour the cold custard into an ice cream maker and churn according to the manufacturer's instructions.

Serve the gelato right away, or spoon it into a freezer-safe container, place parchment or waxed paper directly on the surface, cover tightly, and freeze for up to 3 days.

1 cup sugar

2¼ cups milk

¾ cup light corn syrup

2 pounds cream cheese, cut into pieces at room temperature

2 teaspoons vanilla extract

½ teaspoon salt

MAKES ABOUT 1 QUART

GRAHAM CRACKER SANDWICHES

Sandwich a scoop of Cream Cheese Gelato between graham crackers and freeze.

ice creams and gelatos

FROZEN YOGURTS and SHERBETS

vanilla-berry frozen yogurt 52

MAPLE-BANANA GREEK FROZEN YOGURT 54

HONEY FROZEN YOGURT 55

DULCE DE LECHE FROZEN YOGURT 57

strawberry–crème fraîche sherbet 58

KEY LIME SHERBET 59

CREAMY TANGERINE SHERBET 60

High-quality yogurt enhanced with just the right amount of sweetener and vanilla extract provides the base for this summery delight. Here, instead of spooning berries on top, the berries are crushed and then swirled into the yogurt to spread their fruity flavor throughout.

4 cups plain whole-milk yogurt

⅔ cup plus 2 tablespoons sugar

¼ cup light corn syrup

2 tablespoons vanilla extract

Pinch of salt

½ cup raspberries

½ cup blueberries

½ cup blackberries

1 teaspoon fresh lemon juice

MAKES ABOUT 1½ QUARTS

VANILLA-BERRY FROZEN YOGURT

WITH BARS VARIATION

In a bowl, whisk together the yogurt, the ⅔ cup sugar, the corn syrup, the vanilla, and the salt. Cover and refrigerate until very cold, at least 2 hours or up to 1 day.

In another bowl, combine the raspberries, blueberries, blackberries, lemon juice, and the remaining 2 tablespoons sugar. With a fork, lightly crush the berries until they release some of their juices. Cover the mixture and refrigerate until ready to use.

Pour the cold yogurt mixture into an ice cream maker and churn according to the manufacturer's instructions. As soon as the frozen yogurt has finished churning, spoon half of it into a freezer-safe container. Top with dollops of the reserved berry mixture, using about half of it, and stir gently in a figure eight to swirl the mixture into the yogurt.

Top with the remaining frozen yogurt and then with the remaining berry mixture and again stir in a figure eight to mix.

Place parchment or waxed paper directly on the surface. Cover tightly and freeze until firm, at least 2 hours or up to 3 days.

VANILLA-BERRY FROZEN YOGURT BARS

Pour the churned frozen yogurt into an ice cream bar mold and swirl some berry mixture into each mold. Freeze until solid, at least 4 hours or up to 3 days.

Using bananas in frozen treats is delicious, yet can be somewhat tricky because you must work quickly before the fruit turns brown. Here, golden maple syrup adds depth of flavor.

2 firm but ripe bananas (about 1 pound total weight), peeled

2 cups Greek-style plain whole-milk yogurt

1 cup maple syrup, preferably grade A

½ cup heavy cream

2 teaspoons fresh lemon juice

Pinch salt

MAKES ABOUT 1 QUART

MAPLE-BANANA GREEK FROZEN YOGURT

In a blender or food processor, combine the bananas, yogurt, maple syrup, cream, lemon juice, and salt and process until very smooth. Pour the banana-yogurt mixture into a bowl.

Nest the bowl with the yogurt mixture in an ice bath and stir occasionally until very cold, about 20 minutes. It is important to chill the mixture well to prevent discoloration.

Pour the cold yogurt mixture into an ice cream maker and churn according to the manufacturer's instructions. Spoon the frozen yogurt into a freezer-safe container and place parchment or waxed paper directly on the surface. Cover tightly and freeze until firm, at least 2 hours or up to 3 days.

Lightly tangy yogurt, floral honey, and crunchy poppy seeds combine in this easy-to-prepare frozen yogurt. A touch of heavy cream lends richness to the base, while grated lemon zest and a pinch of salt help these somewhat subtle flavors shine.

HONEY FROZEN YOGURT

WITH POPPY SEEDS

In a bowl, whisk together the yogurt, cream, honey, lemon zest, and salt until smooth. Cover and refrigerate until very cold, at least 2 hours or up to 1 day.

Pour the cold yogurt mixture into an ice cream maker and churn according to the manufacturer's instructions. Spoon the frozen yogurt into a freezer-safe container and place parchment or waxed paper directly on the surface. Cover tightly and freeze until firm, at least 2 hours or up to 3 days.

3 cups plain whole-milk yogurt

1 cup heavy cream

¾ cup wildflower or clover honey

Grated zest of 1 lemon

Pinch salt

MAKES ABOUT 1 QUART

HONEY–POPPY SEED FROZEN YOGURT

Before refrigerating the yogurt mixture, stir in 1 tablespoon poppy seeds. Or, sprinkle 1 tablespoon poppy seeds over the frozen yogurt when serving.

frozen yogurts and sherbets

Dulce de leche, literally "candy of milk," takes time to make but is well worth the wait. As the sweetened milk caramelizes in the oven, it thickens to the texture of a soft caramel candy. When swirled into tangy frozen yogurt, the result is pure dessert bliss. Top each serving with a scattering of caramel corn or nuts, if you like.

DULCE DE LECHE FROZEN YOGURT

To make the dulce de leche, preheat the oven to 400°F. In a 1-quart baking dish, combine the condensed milk and salt. Cover with aluminum foil and place inside a larger baking pan. Place the setup in the oven and carefully pour hot water into the baking pan to reach halfway up the sides of the baking dish. Cook until thickened and darkened to an amber-colored caramel, 1½ to 2 hours. Let cool completely. You should have about 2 cups. Cover and refrigerate 1 cup.

In a bowl whisk together the yogurt, cream, milk, vanilla, and the 1 cup of dulce de leche until smooth. Cover and refrigerate until very cold, at least 2 hours or up to 1 day.

Pour the cold yogurt mixture into an ice cream maker and churn according to the manufacturer's instructions. As soon as it has finished churning, spoon half of it into a freezer-safe container. Top with dollops of the reserved dulce de leche, using about ½ cup, and stir gently in a figure eight to swirl the mixture into the yogurt. Top with the remaining ½ cup dulce de leche and again stir in a figure eight to mix.

Place parchment or waxed paper directly on the surface. Cover tightly and freeze until firm, at least 2 hours or up to 3 days.

2 (14-ounce) cans sweetened condensed milk

¼ teaspoon salt

2 cups Greek-style plain whole-milk yogurt

1 cup heavy cream

½ cup whole milk

1 teaspoon vanilla extract

MAKES ABOUT 1 QUART

frozen yogurts and sherbets

Sherbet is usually made with heavy cream or milk blended with a fruit purée. In this version, crème fraîche replaces the milk or cream, adding a welcome tang to complement the sweet strawberries. A touch of fresh lemon juice helps draw out the berry flavor.

3 cups (1½ pints) strawberries, hulled

2 tablespoons sugar

1 cup crème fraîche

½ cup light corn syrup

2 teaspoons fresh lemon juice

Pinch salt

MAKES ABOUT 1 QUART

STRAWBERRY–CRÈME FRAÎCHE SHERBET

In a bowl, combine the strawberries and sugar and lightly crush the berries with a fork. Whisk in the crème fraîche, corn syrup, lemon juice, and salt. Cover and refrigerate until very cold, at least 2 hours or up to 1 day.

Pour the cold strawberry mixture into an ice cream maker and churn according to the manufacturer's instructions. Spoon the sherbet into a freezer-safe container and place parchment or waxed paper directly on the surface. Cover tightly and freeze until firm, at least 2 hours or up to 3 days.

Tiny, sweet Key limes shine in this sherbet, offset by a measure of sour cream. If you cannot find Key limes, widely available Persian limes can be substituted; they are not as sweet, however, so add 2 tablespoons sugar to the saucepan with the water to compensate for their tartness.

KEY LIME SHERBET

In a saucepan, combine the sugar and ¾ cup water. Bring to a boil over medium-high heat, stirring occasionally until the sugar is completely dissolved and a syrup has formed, about 5 minutes. Let cool to room temperature.

In a bowl, whisk together the lime zest and juice, half-and-half, sour cream, salt, and cooled sugar syrup. Cover and refrigerate until very cold, at least 2 hours or up to 1 day.

Pour the cold lime mixture into an ice cream maker and churn according to the manufacturer's instructions. Spoon the sherbet into a freezer-safe container and place parchment or waxed paper directly on the surface. Cover tightly and freeze until firm, at least 2 hours or up to 3 days.

¾ cup sugar

Finely grated zest of 6 Key limes

½ cup fresh Key lime juice (from about 12 Key limes)

1½ cups half-and-half

½ cup sour cream

Pinch salt

MAKES ABOUT 1 QUART

frozen yogurts and sherbets

This refreshing sherbet turns the elements of a classic childhood ice pop into a sophisticated dessert, bright with the flavor of fresh tangerines. Look for tangerines during the winter months, when they proliferate in local markets. Mandarins, satsumas, or clementines can be substituted.

1 cup heavy cream

1 cup crème fraîche

½ cup light corn syrup

½ cup sugar

Finely grated zest of 2 tangerines

2 cups fresh tangerine juice (from about 10 tangerines)

Pinch salt

MAKES ABOUT 1 QUART

CREAMY TANGERINE SHERBET

WITH TANGERINE-CREAM FLOAT VARIATION

In a bowl, whisk together the cream, crème fraîche, corn syrup, sugar, tangerine zest and juice, and salt. Cover and refrigerate until very cold, at least 2 hours or up to 1 day.

Pour the cold tangerine mixture into an ice cream maker and churn according to the manufacturer's instructions. Spoon the sherbet into a freezer-safe container and place parchment or waxed paper directly on the surface. Cover tightly and freeze until firm, at least 2 hours or up to 3 days.

TANGERINE-CREAM FLOAT

To assemble a float, place a couple scoops of the sherbet in a tall glass and add ¼ cup chilled tangerine soda. Serve with an iced-tea spoon.

SORBETS and GRANITAS

sorbet of mixed melons 64

STRAWBERRY-MINT SORBET 66

BOOZY BLOOD ORANGE GRANITA 67

MANGO-GINGER SORBET 69

vietnamese coffee granita 70

APPLE SPICE SORBET 71

POMEGRANATE GRANITA 72

LIMONCELLO SORBET 75

This refreshing sorbet showcases melons at their summer best. Choose from the sweetest-smelling melon varieties at the market or just pick your favorite. For a refreshing twist, add ¼ cup loosely packed fresh spearmint leaves to the food processor while puréeing the melon mixture.

¾ cup sugar

4 cups diced ripe melon
(from about 1 small melon)

1 tablespoon fresh
lemon juice

Pinch salt

MAKES ABOUT 1½ QUARTS

SORBET OF MIXED MELONS

WITH POPS VARIATION

In a small saucepan, combine the sugar and ¾ cup water. Bring to a boil over medium-high heat, stirring occasionally until the sugar is completely dissolved and a syrup has formed. Let cool to room temperature.

Pour the cooled syrup into a blender or food processor. Add the melon, lemon juice, and salt and blend until very smooth. Pour into a bowl, cover, and refrigerate until very cold, at least 2 hours or up to 1 day.

Pour the cold melon purée into an ice cream maker and churn according to the manufacturer's instructions. Spoon the sorbet into a freezer-safe container and place parchment or waxed paper directly on the surface. Cover tightly and freeze until firm, at least 2 hours or up to 3 days.

**MELON MEDLEY
SORBET POPS**

Churn batches of three different sorbet flavors, such as cantaloupe, honeydew, and watermelon, and then layer them in ice cream bar molds. Freeze until solid, at least 4 hours or up to 3 days.

This thirst-quenching sorbet, which makes the most of seasonal berries, is sublime on a hot summer day. Other fresh herbs, such as basil or lemon verbena, can be substituted for the mint.

STRAWBERRY-MINT SORBET

3 cups (1½ pints) strawberries, hulled and cut in half

⅔ cup sugar

2 tablespoons fresh mint leaves, torn into small pieces or roughly chopped

2 teaspoons fresh lemon juice

Pinch salt

MAKES ABOUT 1 QUART

In a bowl, stir together the strawberries, sugar, and mint leaves. Cover and let stand at room temperature until the berries release some of their juices and the sugar is completely dissolved, about 30 minutes.

Pour the strawberry mixture into a blender or food processor. Add the lemon juice and salt and blend until very smooth. Transfer to a bowl, cover, and refrigerate until cold, at least 2 hours or up to 1 day.

Pour the cold strawberry purée into an ice cream maker and churn according to the manufacturer's instructions. Spoon the sorbet into a freezer-safe container and place parchment or waxed paper directly on the surface. Cover tightly and freeze until firm, at least 2 hours or up to 3 days.

Blood oranges are only available for a few months in the late winter and early spring. When squeezed, their crimson juice produces a gorgeous granita. Serve it with a dollop of Whipped Cream (page 70) for a refreshing dessert.

BOOZY BLOOD ORANGE GRANITA

Combine the blood orange zest, sugar, and ¾ cup water in a small saucepan. Bring to a boil over medium-high heat, stirring occasionally until the sugar is completely dissolved and a syrup has formed, about 5 minutes. Let cool to room temperature.

Pour the cooled syrup into a wide, shallow dish that will easily fit in the freezer. Stir in the blood orange juice, salt, and orange liqueur.

Freeze the mixture until a thin layer of ice forms around the edges and on top, about 1 hour. Using a fork, rake the mixture, breaking up the solid portions into fine flakes of ice. Return the mixture to the freezer and continue to freeze for 2–3 hours longer, scraping the ice crystals with the fork to break them up every 30 minutes. The finished granita should have fine, flaky ice crystals and the consistency of a fluffy sherbet.

If the granita freezes too firmly, remove it from the freezer and let stand at room temperature to soften for 10 minutes, then scrape with the fork until the ice crystals are of even size and return the granita to the freezer. Spoon the finished granita into a freezer-safe container, cover tightly, and freeze for up to 3 days.

Finely grated zest of 2 blood oranges

¾ cup sugar

1¾ cups fresh blood orange juice (from about 6 blood oranges)

Pinch of salt

3 tablespoons orange liqueur such as Grand Marnier or triple sec

MAKES ABOUT 1 QUART

sorbets and granitas

The pungent, spicy flavor of fresh ginger enhances the tropical sweetness of mango in this sorbet. Serve it at the end of an Asian- or Indian-themed meal for a fitting finale. You can garnish with crystallized ginger, cut into slivers, for a beautiful presentation.

MANGO-GINGER SORBET

WITH MARGARITA POPS VARIATION

In a small saucepan, combine the sugar and ¾ cup water. Bring to a boil over medium-high heat, stirring occasionally until the sugar is completely dissolved and a syrup has formed. Let cool to room temperature.

Peel and dice the mangoes, discarding the pits. Place the diced mango in a blender or food processor and add the cooled syrup, ginger, lime juice, and salt. Process until very smooth. Pour into a bowl, cover, and refrigerate until very cold, at least 2 hours or up to 1 day.

Pour the cold mango purée into an ice cream maker and churn according to the manufacturer's instructions. Spoon the sorbet into a freezer-safe container and place parchment or waxed paper directly on the surface. Cover tightly and freeze until firm, at least 2 hours or up to 3 days.

MANGO-GINGER GELATO: Transform this sorbet into a gelato by whisking ¾ cup heavy cream into the mango purée before churning.

¾ cup sugar

2 ripe mangoes (about 2 pounds total weight)

1 tablespoon peeled and grated fresh ginger

2 tablespoons fresh lime juice

Pinch salt

MAKES ABOUT 1 QUART

MANGO-GINGER MARGARITA POPS

Pour the churned sorbet into ice-pop molds and freeze until solid, at least 4 hours or up to 3 days. When ready to serve, unmold, squeeze lime juice on each pop, and sprinkle with a little sea salt.

sorbets and granitas

Vietnamese coffee is typically served with sweetened condensed milk over ice. Here, the coffee itself is transformed into "ice," which is then served over the thick, sugary milk and topped with a dollop of whipped cream. Try it as an innovative dessert for a Southeast Asian meal.

3 cups freshly brewed hot coffee

¼ cup sugar

½ cup sweetened condensed milk

Whipped Cream (see below), for serving (optional)

MAKES ABOUT 1 QUART

VIETNAMESE COFFEE GRANITA

In a wide, shallow dish that will easily fit into the freezer, combine the coffee, sugar, and 1½ cups water. Whisk to dissolve the sugar. Freeze the mixture until a thin layer of ice forms around the edges and on top, about 2 hours.

Using a fork, rake the mixture, breaking up the solid portions into fine flakes of ice. Return the mixture to the freezer and continue to freeze for 2–3 hours longer, scraping the ice crystals with the fork to break them up every 30 minutes. The finished granita should have fine, flaky ice crystals and the consistency of a fluffy sherbet.

If the granita freezes too firmly, remove it from the freezer and let stand at room temperature to soften for 10 minutes, then scrape with the fork until the ice crystals are of even size and return the granita to the freezer. Spoon the finished granita into a freezer-safe container, cover tightly, and freeze for up to 3 days.

To serve, divide the condensed milk evenly among each of 4 serving glasses, and then spoon the granita into the glasses. Top with a dollop of Whipped Cream, if desired.

WHIPPED CREAM: In a deep bowl, combine ¾ cup well-chilled heavy cream, 2 tablespoons sugar, and ½ teaspoon vanilla extract. Using a mixer on high speed, beat until the cream is billowy and soft peaks form, about 2 minutes. Cover and refrigerate until ready to use.

Using tart green apples adds a refreshing tart component to this sorbet. For a sweeter flavor, use sweet apples, such as Fuji or Jonagold, and reduce the lemon juice to 1 teaspoon. For a grown-up version of a caramel apple, substitute hard cider for the regular cider and top scoops of the sorbet with Caramel Sauce (page 90).

APPLE SPICE SORBET

In a saucepan, combine the cider, ½ cup water, sugar, cinnamon stick, allspice, cloves, and nutmeg. Bring to a boil over medium-high heat, stirring occasionally until the sugar is completely dissolved and a syrup has formed, about 5 minutes. Remove from the heat and strain through a fine-mesh sieve placed over a large heatproof bowl. Immediately add the apples and let cool to room temperature. The apples will soften in the hot liquid.

Place the apple mixture in a blender or food processor and process until very smooth. If desired, push the purée through the fine-mesh sieve to remove the bits of apple skins. Pour into a bowl, add the lemon juice, cover, and refrigerate until very cold, at least 2 hours or up to 1 day.

Pour the cold apple spice purée into an ice cream maker and churn according to the manufacturer's instructions. Spoon the sorbet into a freezer-safe container and place parchment or waxed paper directly on the surface. Cover tightly and freeze until firm, at least 2 hours or up to 3 days.

2½ cups filtered cider or apple juice

½ cup sugar

1 cinnamon stick

2 whole allspice

2 whole cloves

Pinch of freshly grated nutmeg

5 tart green apples such as Granny Smith (about 2½ pounds total weight), cored and cut into 1-inch cubes

1 tablespoon fresh lemon juice

MAKES ABOUT 1 QUART

sorbets and granitas

High-quality pomegranate juice is readily available in markets today. Its lightly sweet, slightly peppery flavor makes an intriguing dessert, brightened with a touch of fresh lime juice. Try it in bowls topped with fresh pomegranate seeds, or make it into ice pop.

¾ cup sugar

3 cups pure pomegranate juice

Pinch salt

1 tablespoon fresh lime juice

MAKES ABOUT 1 QUART

POMEGRANATE GRANITA

WITH POPS VARIATION

In a small saucepan, combine the sugar and ½ cup water. Bring to a boil over medium-high heat, stirring occasionally until the sugar is completely dissolved and a syrup has formed. Let cool to room temperature.

Pour the syrup into a bowl and stir in the pomegranate juice, salt, and lime juice. Cover and refrigerate until very cold, at least 2 hours or up to 1 day.

Pour the cold pomegranate mixture into a wide, shallow dish that will easily fit into the freezer. Freeze until a thin layer of ice forms around the edges and on top, about 1 hour. Using a fork, rake the mixture, breaking up the solid portions into fine flakes of ice. Return the mixture to the freezer and continue to freeze for 2–3 hours longer, scraping the ice crystals with the fork to break them up every 30 minutes. The finished granita should have fine, flaky ice crystals and the consistency of a fluffy sherbet.

If the granita freezes too firmly, remove it from the freezer and let stand at room temperature to soften for 10 minutes, then scrape with the fork until the ice crystals are of even size and return the granita to the freezer. Spoon the finished granita into a freezer-safe container, cover tightly, and freeze for up to 3 days.

POMEGRANATE ICE POPS

Instead of pouring the pomegranate mixture into a shallow dish, pour it into ice-pop molds and freeze until solid, at least 4 hours or up to 3 days.

An ideal palate cleanser at the end of a meal, this bright lemony sorbet will have you yearning for more. The addition of Limoncello, a lemon liqueur from southern Italy, transforms a seemingly ordinary lemon sorbet into something sophisticated.

LIMONCELLO SORBET

In a saucepan, combine the sugar and 2 cups water. Bring to a boil over medium-high heat, stirring occasionally until the sugar is completely dissolved and a syrup has formed, about 5 minutes. Let the syrup cool to room temperature.

Pour the syrup into a bowl and stir in the lemon zest and juice, salt, and limoncello. Cover and refrigerate until very cold, at least 2 hours or up to 1 day.

Pour the cold lemon mixture into an ice cream maker and churn according to the manufacturer's instructions. Spoon the sorbet into a freezer-safe container and place parchment or waxed paper directly on the surface. Cover tightly and freeze until firm, at least 2 hours or up to 3 days.

LEMON BOWLS: Using a paring knife, trim off about ¾ inch from the stem end of 8 lemons. You need an opening about 1¼ inches in diameter. Using a teaspoon, hollow out the flesh and membranes from each lemon capturing the juice in the bowl. Put the removed lemon flesh in a fine-mesh sieve and press against it with the back of a spoon to extract the juice. Use the juice for making the sorbet (you will need ½ cup) or reserve for another use. Trim a thin slice from the bottom end of each lemon so it will stand upright.

Line a baking sheet with parchment or waxed paper, transfer the hollowed-out lemons to the baking sheet, and freeze until cold, at least 20 minutes. Fill each chilled lemon bowl with about ½ cup of the sorbet, mounding it on top and pressing firmly with a teaspoon. The filled bowls will keep in the freezer for up to 1 day.

1½ cups sugar

Finely grated zest of 2 lemons

½ cup fresh lemon juice

Pinch salt

½ cup limoncello

MAKES ABOUT 1 QUART

sorbets and granitas

CONES, COOKIES, SAUCES and TOPPINGS

waffle cones 79

GLUTEN-FREE WAFFLE CONES 80

CREPE CONES 83

CHOCOLATE CHIP COOKIES 84

fudgy brownies 85

CONFETTI COOKIES 86

TUILE COOKIES 88

FRESH STRAWBERRY TOPPING 89

hot fudge sauce 89

CARAMEL SAUCE 91

MARSHMALLOW CREAM TOPPING 92

SPICED PEPITAS 94

brandied cherries 95

SUGARED NUTS 95

HOMEMADE SPRINKLES 96

The easiest way to make waffle cones is by using a machine specifically designed for the job. Waffle cone makers are inexpensive, and most come with a mode that makes shaping the cones a snap. A pizelle iron can be used instead.

WAFFLE CONES

AND WAFFLE CUPS

In a bowl, combine the eggs and granulated and brown sugars. Whisk vigorously until the mixture lightens in color and is smooth, about 1 minute. Whisk in the melted butter, salt, vanilla, and flour until completely combined. Cover and refrigerate for at least 30 minutes or up to 3 days before using.

Make the cones in a waffle cone maker according to the manufacturer's instructions. Let cool completely on a wire rack. Use right away, or store in an airtight container at room temperature for up to 3 days.

2 large eggs

⅓ cup granulated sugar

⅓ cup packed light brown sugar

4 tablespoons unsalted butter, melted

¼ teaspoon salt

2 teaspoons vanilla extract

¾ cup all-purpose flour

MAKES ABOUT 12 CONES

WAFFLE CUPS

To make waffle cups, follow the manufacturer's instructions for making waffle cones, adding about half the amount of batter to the iron as directed. Remove the baked waffle round from the iron and carefully drape it over the outside of an overturned bowl, pressing it to the sides of the bowl (it's okay if the sides pinch or buckle). Let the waffle cup cool on the bowl until firm.

cones, cookies, sauces, and toppings

Look for gluten-free flour in the baking aisle of supermarkets. Using a brand that can be substituted for regular all-purpose flour in the exact amount is ideal for this recipe. Cup4Cup is a great choice and contains some milk powder, which adds a lightness to the texture. If using a gluten-free flour that does not include xanthan gum, add a ¼ teaspoon per cup of flour.

GLUTEN-FREE WAFFLE CONES

WITH CHOCOLATE EDGE

2 large eggs

⅓ cup granulated sugar

⅓ cup packed light brown sugar

4 tablespoons unsalted butter, melted

¼ teaspoon salt

2 teaspoons vanilla extract

¾ cup gluten-free all-purpose flour

MAKES ABOUT 1 QUART

In a bowl, combine the eggs and granulated and brown sugars. Whisk vigorously until the mixture lightens in color and is smooth, about 1 minute. Whisk in the melted butter, salt, vanilla, and flour until completely combined. Cover and refrigerate for at least 30 minutes or up to 3 days before using.

Make the cones in a waffle cone maker according to the manufacturer's instructions. Let cool completely on a wire rack. Use right away, or store in an airtight container at room temperature for up to 3 days.

CHOCOLATE-EDGED CONES

Line a baking sheet with parchment or waxed paper. Dip the edge of each waffle cone into warm melted semisweet chocolate and place on the prepared pan. If desired, coat the edges with chopped toasted nuts or sprinkles. Refrigerate until the chocolate is firm, about 10 minutes, before using.

cones, cookies, sauces, and toppings

To make cones, you will need to cook the crepes until golden all over, as opposed to simply golden on the edges as when making a traditional crepe. This will ensure the crepes will firm up crisply as they cool in a cone shape. It is also important that the crepe is very thin, otherwise it's less likely to hold once cool.

CREPE CONES

In a large bowl, whisk together the eggs and 1¾ cups milk. Slowly add the flour, sugar, and salt, whisking constantly to avoid lumps. Cover and refrigerate for 2 hours. When ready to cook, stir the batter well. It should be the consistency of heavy cream. If it is too thick, thin with a little more milk.

Heat a 6-inch nonstick frying pan or crepe pan with low, sloping sides over medium-high heat. Add about 1 teaspoon of the butter. Tilt the pan from side to side to coat the bottom with the butter as it melts. Pour about ¼ cup of the batter into the pan, quickly tilting and swirling the pan to coat the bottom evenly with the batter. Pour any excess batter back into the bowl and return the pan to the heat. Cook until the center of the crepe bubbles and the edges begin to dry, about 30 seconds. Using tongs, turn the crepe and cook until golden on the second side, about 20 seconds. Transfer the crepe to a flat plate. Repeat with the remaining batter, adding about 1 teaspoon butter to the pan before cooking each crepe and stacking the crepes, separated with a small piece of parchment or waxed paper, as they are ready. (At this point, the crepes can be covered and refrigerated for up to 2 days before continuing.)

Preheat the oven to 350°F.

Arrange the crepes in a single layer on a baking sheet, transfer to the oven, and bake just until the edges are crisp and the center feels dry to the touch, about 12–15 minutes. Remove from the oven. While each crepe is still warm and flexible, wrap it around a waffle cone mold and let cool completely. The crepe will firm up as it cools. Cook, bake, and shape the remaining crepes the same way. The cones are best eaten the same day they are baked.

4 large eggs

1¾ cups whole milk, or as needed

⅓ cup all-purpose flour

2 tablespoons sugar

½ teaspoon salt

About 4 tablespoons unsalted butter

MAKES ABOUT 24 CONES

cones, cookies, sauces, and toppings

There's no better accompaniment to a bowl of ice cream or gelato than a homemade chocolate chip cookie. You can also use the cookies to make ice cream sandwiches—either full-size or miniature—for frozen treats to eat out of hand.

CHOCOLATE CHIP COOKIES

1⅓ cups all-purpose flour

½ teaspoon baking powder

½ teaspoon baking soda

½ teaspoon salt

½ cup unsalted butter, at room temperature

½ cup granulated sugar

½ cup packed light brown sugar

1 large egg

1 teaspoon vanilla extract

1 cup semisweet chocolate chips

MAKES ABOUT 48 COOKIES

Preheat the oven to 350°F. In a bowl, stir together the flour, baking powder, baking soda, and salt and set aside.

Using an electric mixer on high speed, beat the butter until fluffy and pale yellow. Add the granulated and brown sugars and continue beating until the mixture is well blended, about 1 minute. Add the egg and vanilla and beat on low speed until completely incorporated, stopping to scrape down the sides of the bowl with a rubber spatula as needed.

Add the flour mixture to the butter-sugar mixture and mix on low speed just until blended. Use a wooden spoon to stir in the chocolate chips.

Drop rounded tablespoons of the dough onto 2 ungreased baking sheets, spacing the cookies about 2 inches apart.

Bake the cookies until golden brown around the edges and lightly golden in the center, about 12 minutes, rotating the sheets 180 degrees about halfway through the baking time. Let the cookies cool on the pans on wire racks for about 5 minutes, then transfer the cookies directly to the racks and let cool completely. Serve the cookies right away, or store in an airtight container at room temperature for up to 5 days.

These chewy, fudgy brownies are intensely chocolaty because the batter includes both melted chocolate and chocolate chips. Other kinds of chips or candy chunks can be substituted for the semisweet chocolate chips. Serve these brownies alongside ice cream, gelato, or frozen yogurt.

FUDGY BROWNIES

Preheat the oven to 350°F. Lightly grease an 8-inch square baking pan.

In a heatproof bowl, combine the butter and chopped chocolate. Set the bowl over (but not touching) simmering water in a saucepan and stir occasionally until melted, about 4 minutes. Remove the bowl from over the heat and add the sugar and salt and stir well with a wooden spoon. Add the eggs and vanilla and stir until well blended. Sift the flour over the mixture and stir until just blended. Stir in the chocolate chips.

Pour the batter into the prepared pan, spreading it evenly and smoothing the top with a long, thin spatula. Bake the brownies until a toothpick inserted into the center comes out almost clean, about 35 minutes. Let the brownies cool completely in the pan on a wire rack.

When ready to serve, cut into 16 small squares and lift out the brownies with an offset spatula.

½ cup unsalted butter, cut into 4 pieces

3 ounces unsweetened chocolate, finely chopped

1 cup sugar

Pinch salt

2 large eggs, at room temperature

1 teaspoon vanilla extract

¾ cup cake flour

¾ cup semisweet chocolate chips

MAKES 16 BROWNIES

Using these cookies, which have a cakelike texture, for making ice cream sandwiches unites cake and ice cream in a creative, new way. Plus, the addition of sprinkles to the batter will give the sandwiches a festive air.

1½ cups all-purpose flour

⅛ teaspoon baking powder

⅛ teaspoon baking soda

⅛ teaspoon salt

6 tablespoons unsalted butter, at room temperature

¼ cup vegetable shortening

½ cup plus 2 tablespoons sugar

1 large egg plus 1 large egg yolk

1½ teaspoons vanilla extract

2 tablespoons heavy cream

½ cup multicolored sprinkles, homemade (page 96) or store-bought

MAKES ABOUT 12 COOKIES

CONFETTI COOKIES

Preheat the oven to 350°F. In a bowl, stir together the flour, baking powder, baking soda, and salt and set aside.

Using an electric mixture on high speed, beat the butter, shortening, and sugar until fluffy and light, about 3 minutes. Add the whole egg, egg yolk, and vanilla and beat on low speed until completely incorporated, stopping to scrape down the sides of the bowl with a rubber spatula as needed.

Add the flour mixture to the butter-sugar mixture and mix on low speed just until blended, then mix in the cream. Use a wooden spoon to stir in the sprinkles.

Drop rounded tablespoons of the dough onto 2 ungreased baking sheets, spacing the cookies about 2 inches apart.

Bake the cookies until golden brown around the edges and lightly golden in the center, about 12 minutes, rotating the sheets 180 degrees halfway through the baking time. Let the cookies cool briefly on the pans on wire racks for about 5 minutes, then transfer the cookies directly to the racks and let cool completely.

Serve the cookies right away, or store in an airtight container at room temperature for up to 5 days.

cones, cookies, sauces, and toppings

These delicate cookies are the perfect crunchy partner for a bowl of ice cream or other frozen treat. You can use two cookies to make a sandwich or use one cookie as a base on which to build a composed dessert. You can also make delicious cookie cups from the same batter (see below).

TUILE COOKIES

4 tablespoons
unsalted butter

¼ cup light corn syrup

¼ cup sugar

¼ cup all-purpose flour

Pinch salt

MAKES ABOUT 12 COOKIES

Preheat the oven to 350°F. Line 3 large baking sheets with silicone baking mats or parchment paper.

In a small saucepan, combine the butter, corn syrup, and sugar. Bring to a boil over medium heat, stirring occasionally until the sugar dissolves. Remove from the heat and whisk in the flour and salt until combined. Let cool completely, about 30 minutes.

Use a measuring tablespoon, scoop a heaping spoonful of the batter from the saucepan and drop it onto one of the prepared baking sheets. Repeat, filling each baking sheet with 4 evenly spaced scoops of batter. Bake the cookies, 1 sheet at a time, until golden, about 10 minutes. Let cool just until the edges are set, 1–2 minutes. Using an offset spatula, transfer the cookies to a wire rack and let cool completely.

Serve the cookies right away, or carefully place in an airtight container and store at room temperature for up to 3 days.

TUILE COOKIE CUPS: As soon as the cookies come out of the oven, use a small offset spatula to lift each cookie off of the pan and carefully press it into the cup of a muffin pan. Let cool in the muffin pan to room temperature, then carefully remove each cookie cup from the pan.

This is a great sauce to make in the summer when strawberries are at their peak. Blending most of the strawberry mixture until smooth, then mixing in chopped berries produces a sauce that coats frozen desserts evenly but also has juicy berry bits.

FRESH STRAWBERRY TOPPING

In a bowl, stir together the strawberries, sugar, and lemon juice. Spoon all but ½ cup of the strawberry mixture into a blender and blend until smooth. Stir the strawberry purée into the reserved chopped strawberry mixture. Use right away, or cover and store in the refrigerator for up to 3 days.

4 cups (2 pints) strawberries, hulled and coarsely chopped

⅓ cup sugar

1 teaspoon fresh lemon juice

MAKES ABOUT 3 CUPS

Warm, gooey chocolate sauce poured over vanilla ice cream is the ultimate simple pleasure, but this deep, rich, chocolaty sauce complements any frozen treat.

HOT FUDGE SAUCE

In a small, heavy saucepan, combine the cream, corn syrup, and brown sugar. Bring to a boil over medium-low heat, stirring occasionally until the sugar dissolves, about 5 minutes.

In a heatproof bowl, combine the chocolate and salt. Pour the hot cream mixture over the chocolate and stir with a silicone spatula until the chocolate is melted and smooth. Stir in the vanilla.

Use right away, or let cool, cover, and refrigerate for up to 6 days. Reheat gently over low heat before serving (you may need to thin it with a little cream).

⅔ cup heavy cream

½ cup light corn syrup

2 tablespoons firmly packed dark brown sugar

5 ounces bittersweet chocolate, coarsely chopped

Pinch salt

1 teaspoon vanilla extract

MAKES ABOUT 2 CUPS

cones, cookies, sauces, and toppings

Silky, buttery caramel sauce poured on almost anything is divine. Or, try swirling this sauce into vanilla or chocolate ice cream during the last few minutes of churning.

CARAMEL SAUCE

WITH SALTED VARIATION

In a heavy, deep saucepan, cook the sugar over medium-high heat until it begins to melt around the edges, about 5 minutes. Continue to cook, stirring with a wooden spoon, until the sugar is melted and turns a golden amber, about 3 minutes longer.

Carefully pour the cream down the side of the pan in a slow, steady stream (it will bubble and spatter), stirring constantly until completely smooth. Stir in the salt. Pour the sauce into a small heatproof bowl and let cool completely before using.

Use right away, or cover and store in the refrigerator for up to 1 week. Bring the sauce to room temperature before serving.

1½ cups sugar
1¼ cups heavy cream
Pinch salt

MAKES ABOUT 2½ CUPS

SALTED CARAMEL SAUCE

Omit the pinch of salt. After pouring the cream down the side of the pan, stir in ½ cup unsalted butter and 1 teaspoon coarse sea salt. Pour the caramel sauce into a small heatproof bowl and let cool completely before using.

cones, cookies, sauces, and toppings

This sweet, fluffy topping is a crowd-pleaser. For a deconstructed rocky road ice cream, spoon dollops of this topping onto scoops of Rich Chocolate Ice Cream (page 27) and sprinkle with chopped nuts. For a decadent topping, swirl the marshmallow cream with Hot Fudge Sauce (page 89).

2 large egg whites

1 cup miniature marshmallows

1 cup sugar

¼ cup light corn syrup

½ teaspoon cream of tartar

Pinch salt

1 teaspoon vanilla extract

MAKES ABOUT 5 CUPS, ENOUGH TO COAT 8 TO 10 ICE CREAM CONES

TORCHED MARSHMALLOW TOPPING

Using a small offset spatula, spread about ⅓ cup Marshmallow Cream Topping over the surface of scooped ice cream. Use gentle figure-eight sweeping motions to create peaks and valleys of marshmallow. Using a kitchen torch and a sweeping motion, carefully brown the marshmallow until golden.

MARSHMALLOW CREAM TOPPING

WITH TORCHED VARIATION

In a large, clean, heatproof bowl, combine the egg whites, marshmallows, sugar, corn syrup, cream of tartar, salt, and 6 tablespoons water. Set the bowl over (but not touching) simmering water in a saucepan and whisk constantly until the sugar and marshmallows have dissolved and the mixture is very warm to the touch (about 160°F on an instant-read thermometer), about 3 minutes. Remove the bowl from the saucepan.

Using an electric mixer on medium-high speed, beat the mixture until soft peaks form, about 2 minutes. Reduce the mixer speed to low and beat in the vanilla. Use right away.

Pepitas, "pumpkin seeds" in Spanish, are the tender green interiors of the white hulled seeds of pumpkins (or squashes). Here, they are tossed with spices, sugar, and honey then toasted to yield a crunch, sweet-savory topping or mix-in for ice cream, gelato, frozen yogurt, or sherbet.

2 cups pumpkin seeds

3 tablespoons sugar

1 tablespoon honey

2 teaspoons ground cinnamon

1 teaspoon ground ginger

½ teaspoon ground allspice

Pinch freshly grated nutmeg

½ teaspoon freshly ground black pepper

Pinch salt

2 tablespoons unsalted butter, cut into small pieces

MAKES ABOUT 2 CUPS

SPICED PEPITAS

Preheat oven to 350°F. In a bowl, toss together the pumpkin seeds, sugar, honey, cinnamon, ginger, allspice, nutmeg, pepper, and salt. Spread the mixture in a single layer on a rimmed baking sheet. Scatter the butter pieces over the seeds and stir gently to mix.

Bake, stirring the seeds and shaking the pan several times, until lightly browned, 10–12 minutes. If you prefer darker, toaster seeds, bake them for 2–3 minutes longer.

Transfer the seeds to a clean baking sheet and let cool completely. Use right away, or store in an airtight container at room temperature for up to 3 days.

Transform a sundae into an elegant, grown-up presentation by spooning a handful of these tart cherries and some of the brandy syrup over the top. These preserved cherries get better with age. Swirl them into Rich Chocolate Ice Cream (page 27) for a Black Forest frozen treat.

BRANDIED CHERRIES

In a saucepan, combine the granulated and brown sugars, lemon zest, vanilla bean pod and seeds, allspice, salt, and ¾ cup water. Bring to a boil over medium-high heat, stirring occasionally until the sugar is completely dissolved and the mixture becomes more syrupy, about 5 minutes. Remove from the heat, add the cherries, brandy, and vanilla and let stand until cool.

Transfer to a jar, cover tightly, and refrigerate for at least 3 days before serving. The cherries will keep refrigerated for up to 6 months.

½ cup granulated sugar

¼ cup packed dark brown sugar

Zest of 1 lemon, in narrow strips

1 vanilla bean, split in half lengthwise, seeds scraped

4 whole allspice

Pinch of salt

1 pound fresh or frozen dark sweet cherries, stems and pits removed

½ cup brandy

1 teaspoon vanilla extract

MAKES ABOUT 2 PINTS

These nuts will add crunchy texture and a little salt to any sundae. You can substitute cashews, almonds, pistachios or a mixture of nuts for the walnuts.

SUGARED NUTS

Preheat the oven to 350°F. In a bowl, toss together the nuts, sugar, and salt. Spread the mixture in a single layer on a rimmed baking sheet. Scatter the butter pieces over the nuts and stir gently to mix.

Bake, stirring the nuts and shaking the pan several times, until lightly browned, 10–12 minutes. If you prefer darker, toastier nuts, bake them for 2–3 minutes longer.

Transfer the nuts to a clean baking sheet and let cool completely. Use right away, or store in an airtight container at room temperature for up to 3 days.

2 cups walnut halves

3 tablespoons sugar

Pinch salt

2½ tablespoons unsalted butter, cut into small pieces

MAKES ABOUT 2 CUPS

cones, cookies, sauces, and toppings

To make sprinkles, all you need to do is to whip up a batch of old-fashioned royal icing (commonly used for decorating cookies), pipe it into thin strands, and then let them set. Use gel paste, rather than liquid food coloring, if possible, as the colors will be more vibrant and you will not thin the icing as much.

HOMEMADE SPRINKLES

2 cups confectioners' sugar, sifted

1½ tablespoons meringue powder

¼ teaspoon extract such as vanilla or almond (optional)

Food coloring, preferably gel paste type, in color(s) of choice (optional)

MAKES ABOUT ½ CUP (1 OUNCE), ENOUGH TO TOP ABOUT 12 SUNDAES

Line 2 baking sheets with parchment or waxed paper.

In a bowl, combine the sugar, meringue powder, 3 tablespoons warm water, and the extract, if using. Using an electric mixer on medium speed, beat until the mixture is fluffy yet dense, 7–8 minutes.

If you are making sprinkles of different colors, divide the icing into as many small bowls as colors you will be using. If using gel-type coloring, twirl a toothpick into the gel and then twirl the toothpick into the icing until the color is evenly mixed. If a deeper shade is desired, add more gel, a tiny bit at a time. If using liquid-type coloring, add 1 or 2 drops to the icing and mix well, then add additional drops as needed to achieve the desired shade.

To test if the icing is a good consistency for piping, scoop up a spoonful and drizzle it back into the bowl. It should remain in a ribbon on the surface. To thin the icing, using a rubber spatula, stir in warm water, ¼ teaspoon at a time.

Spoon the icing into a pastry bag fitted with a ⅛-inch plain tip. Pipe the icing in straight lines onto the prepared baking sheets. Let the icing dry at room temperature until crisp, about 24 hours. Using a knife, cut strands into desired-size pieces. Use right away, or store in an airtight container at room temperature for up to 1 week.

SUNDAE PARTY

Sundaes can be customized, making them the perfect party food. You just choose a base, a favorite ice cream flavor, and a mix of toppings and you have a memorable, one-of-a-kind treat. These delicious concoctions, whether sandwiched between banana halves, sitting in a waffle bowl, or served on a fudgy brownie, are a good choice for nearly any occasion, from a playdate to a birthday celebration to a dinner party, and for every age group, from kindergartners to grown-ups. Here are some combinations to get you started on putting together your own ice cream sundae bar. If you're a sundae purist, don't forget the whipped cream and cherries.

the formula

BROWNIES, COOKIES, OR CONES + **YOUR FAVORITE SCOOPS** + **MIX OF TOPPINGS**

1 PEACHES & CREAM SUNDAE
Waffle bowls (page 78) + Honey–Poppy Seed Frozen Yogurt (page 55) + sliced peaches + Whipped Cream (page 70)

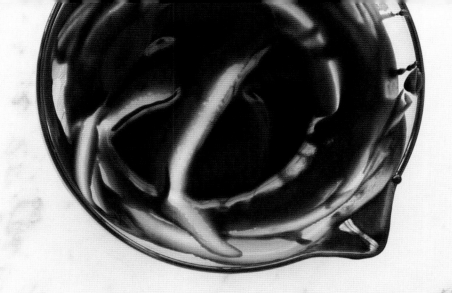

2 MODERN STRAWBERRY SUNDAE

*Fudgy Brownies (page 85) + Balsamic Strawberry
Ice Cream (page 23) + Brandied Cherries (page 95)*

3 DOUBLE-CARAMEL CREPE SUNDAE

*Crepes (page 83) hot from the pan topped with
Dulce de Leche Frozen Yogurt (page 57)
+ Salted Caramel Sauce (page 90)*

4 SIMPLE & PLAYFUL SUNDAE

*Tuile Cookie Cups (page 88) + Vanilla Bean
Ice Cream (page 26) + Homemade Sprinkles (page 96)*

5 THE ULTIMATE SUNDAE

*Fudgy Brownies (page 85) + Rich Chocolate Ice Cream (page 27)
+ Salted Caramel Sauce (page 90) + Marshmallow Cream Topping
(page 93) + Sugared Nuts (page 95)*

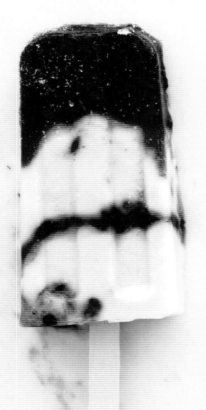

POP & ICE CREAM SANDWICH PARTY

Homemade ice cream sandwiches start with big scoops of your favorite flavor sandwiched between freshly baked cookies. Roll the exposed ice cream edges through crushed candy or nuts for flavor and crunch, or dip half of the sandwich in melted chocolate for extra richness. You can dip ice pops in the same melted chocolate and crushed toppings: just freeze your favorite sherbet, frozen yogurt, or granita in ice-pop molds, unmold, dip in your choice of toppings, and enjoy!

the formula

| YOUR FAVORITE FROZEN BASE | + | COOKIES OR ICE-POP MOLDS | + | CRUSHED TOPPINGS & SAUCES |

1 BLACK & WHITE
Sandwich 1 scoop Vanilla Bean Ice Cream (page 26) between 2 Chocolate Chip Cookies (page 84); dip half of the sandwich in Hot Fudge Sauce (page 89) + coat in crushed Sugared Nuts (page 95)

2 CELEBRATION SANDWICH

Sandwich 1 scoop White Chocolate–Pretzel Gelato (page 47) between 2 Confetti Cookies (page 86); roll the exposed ice cream in Homemade Sprinkles (page 96)

3 DECONSTRUCTED BANANA SPLIT

Top 1 Fudgy Brownie (page 85) with Maple-Banana Greek Frozen Yogurt (page 54) + Fresh Strawberry Topping (page 89) + Whipped Cream (page 70)

4 STRAWBERRY CRUSH POPS

Unmold Strawberry–Créme Fraîche Sherbet pops (page 58) and run them briefly under warm water; dip in crushed salted almonds + shredded sweetened coconut and return to the freezer for 10 minutes before serving

5 KEY LIME PIE POP

Unmold Key Lime Sherbet pops (page 59), dip in fresh lime juice + crushed graham crackers and return to the freezer for 10 minutes before serving

FLOAT BAR

Here's the winning formula for the perfect float: plunk giant scoops of ice cream into a spritzy soda or other fizzy drink, coffee, sparkling wine, or beer and drizzle with something saucy and sweet. You can surprise your friends with unexpected combos, such as Espresso Chip Ice Cream and stout. Pick a favorite from the ideas that follow, or set out a wide array of options and let guests create their own. Add 2 scoops of ice cream for every 1¼ cups liquid, and don't forget long spoons or straws for stirring.

the formula

YOUR FAVORITE FROZEN BASE + **CARBONATED BEVERAGE** + **SWEET SAUCES & GARNISHES**

1 CLASSIC ROOT BEER FLOAT
Root Beer + Vanilla Bean Ice Cream (page 26); top with Whipped Cream (page 70)

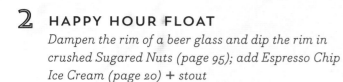

2 HAPPY HOUR FLOAT

Dampen the rim of a beer glass and dip the rim in crushed Sugared Nuts (page 95); add Espresso Chip Ice Cream (page 20) + stout

3 COFFEE BREAK

Chilled coffee + Espresso Chip Ice Cream (page 20); top with Hot Fudge Sauce (page 89)

4 NOT YOUR DAD'S ICE CREAM SODA

Seltzer + Rich Chocolate Ice Cream (page 27) + dash of half-and-half + Hot Fudge Sauce (page 89); top with Whipped Cream (page 70) + Brandied Cherries (page 95)

5 BOOZY CITRUS FLOAT

Blood Orange Granita (page 67) + sparkling wine + zest from 1 orange

SHAKE PARTY

Frothy and thick, sweet and creamy, smooth and rich—a great milkshake is hard to resist. Delicious milkshakes call for no more than three basic ingredients, which are whirled together briefly in a blender. When made with homemade ice creams, syrups, and garnishes, these classic soda fountain drinks scale new flavor heights. Pull out the blender, some tall glasses, and a handful of decorative straws and host a milk shake party! For each milkshake, use 2 scoops of ice cream and 1¼ cups liquid.

the formula

YOUR FAVORITE FROZEN BASE + **COLD DRINK** + **SYRUPS & GARNISHES**

1 AFTER-SCHOOL SPECIAL
Blend whole milk + Salted Peanut Butter & Jelly Ice Cream (page 38); garnish with Whipped Cream (page 70) + 1 Tuile Cookie (page 88)

2 ORANGE CREAM SHAKE
Blend whole milk + 1 scoop Vanilla Bean Ice Cream (page 26) + 1 scoop Orange-Cardamom Ice Cream (page 36); garnish with orange zest

3 GREEN TEA–CHOCOLATE SHAKE
Blend chilled green tea + Green Tea Ice Cream with Chocolate Slivers (page 40) + Hot Fudge Sauce (page 89)

4 LOCO FOR COCO SHAKE
Blend coconut milk + Chocolate Coconut Gelato (page 43) + crumbled Fudgy Brownie (page 85)

5 DOUBLE APPLE SHAKE
Blend apple cider + Apple Spice Sorbet (page 71) + Caramel Sauce (page 90); garnish with apple slices

6 WHITE CHOCOLATE SHAKE
Blend whole milk + White Chocolate Gelato (page 47) + crumbled Confetti Cookies (page 86)

INDEX

index

weldonowen

415 Jackson Street, Suite 200, San Francisco, CA 94111
www.weldonowen.com

THE ICE CREAMERY COOKBOOK
Conceived and produced by Weldon Owen, Inc.
In collaboration with Williams-Sonoma, Inc.
3250 Van Ness Avenue, San Francisco, CA 94109

A WELDON OWEN PRODUCTION

Copyright © 2014 Weldon Owen, Inc.
and Williams-Sonoma, Inc.
All rights reserved, including the right of reproduction
in whole or in part in any form.

Printed and bound in China by 1010 Printing, Ltd.

First printed in 2014
10 9 8 7 6 5 4

Library of Congress Control Number:
2014931493

ISBN 13: 978-1-61628-684-2
ISBN 10: 1-61628-684-9

Weldon Owen is a division of
BONNIER

WELDON OWEN, INC.
CEO and President Terry Newell
VP, Sales and Marketing Amy Kaneko
VP, Publisher Roger Shaw

Associate Publisher Amy Marr
Assistant Editor Emma Rudolph

Creative Director Kelly Booth
Art Director Ashley Lima
Designer Rachel Lopez Metzger

Production Director Chris Hemesath
Associate Production Director Michelle Duggan

Photographer Erin Kunkel
Food Stylist Robyn Valarik
Prop Stylist Emma Star Jensen

ACKNOWLEDGMENTS
Weldon Owen wishes to thank the following people for their generous support in producing this book:
David Bornfriend, Alicia Deal, Elizabeth Parson, and Sharon Silva